Jesse Beaufort Hurlbert

Britain and Her Colonies

Jesse Beaufort Hurlbert

Britain and Her Colonies

ISBN/EAN: 9783337230852

Printed in Europe, USA, Canada, Australia, Japan

Cover: Foto ©ninafisch / pixelio.de

More available books at **www.hansebooks.com**

BRITAIN AND HER COLONIES.

BY

J. BEAUFORT HURLBURT, M.A., LL.D.

MEMBER OF THE CONVOCATION OF THE UNIVERSITY OF TORONTO; FOR SOME TIME PROFESSOR
OF GREEK AND LATIN IN THE UNIVERSITY OF VICTORIA COLLEGE, COBOURG;
CANADIAN COMMISSIONER AND JUROR AT THE INTERNATIONAL
EXHIBITION, LONDON, 1862.

LONDON:
EDWARD STANFORD, 6, CHARING CROSS.
1865.

The right of translation is reserved.

PREFACE.

QUESTIONS of colonial policy and of colonial empire have recently occupied the attention of public men in England more than at any previous time. This has been shown by discussions in Parliament and in the press, and by the Reports of Committees of the House of Commons.

Some of the topics brought most prominently into view have been the cost, defence, and advantages or disadvantages of colonies, the commercial policy of the chief dependencies of the Empire, as at variance with that of England, the relations which those great Commonwealths now sustain towards this country and towards each other, and what changes, if any, should be effected in such relations.

The interest so generally shown in questions of such importance to the various members of the Empire has suggested this treatise.

A brief sketch is given of the chief colonial Empires of ancient and modern times with reference to the civil and commercial policy of the parent States, as far as they throw light upon the colonial policy of Great Britain.

Original sources of information in the debates in Parliament, Reports of Committees, and official documents in public offices and in the British Museum, have invariably been resorted to where necessary; yet the author has not been unmindful of the current opinions of the day in well-informed circles, both commercial and political, on the many controverted questions, Imperial and colonial, here referred to.

The writer has tried to compress into as small a compass as possible the great number and variety of facts connected with colonial history in ancient and modern times, which he has found it necessary to introduce; but for the purpose of illustrating other points, he has sometimes preferred to repeat a reference rather than to multiply quotations.

The question between England and her colonies ought not to be one of separation but of sounder relations, as alike the interest of both, and the interest of good government throughout the world.

In conclusion the author has the pleasing duty of tendering his thanks to those gentlemen, in and out of the public offices, who have so politely aided him in his researches.

LONDON: 1865.

CONTENTS.

CHAPTER I.

GOVERNMENT OF THE FIRST ENGLISH COLONIES.

First permanent English settlement in America, Virginia—The two centres of American colonization, Virginia and New England, differing in their origin and their development—First representative body in America: its composition—A written constitution the model for others—The governor: how appointed—General assembly, courts of justice, corporation dissolved (1624)—First settlers in New England: the origin and character of their government—Plymouth Colony: their charter, its loss—New charter by James I. (1620)—Boundaries of New England—Charter from Charles I. (1628)—Massachusetts: its government, how elected—Court for the transaction of business—Four general assemblies—No reference to religious questions—First church—Oath of supremacy—Charter removed to New England (1629)—Growth of colony—Struggle between the Crown and colony—Loss of charter (1684)—Pure democracy—Representative government not provided for in charter—One house only, then two—From 1684 to 1691 without a charter—One granted by William and Mary (1691) to Massachusetts—Bay: extent, nature of, enlarged powers: less democratic—Blackstone's division of colonies—Provincial, proprietary, and charter governments—Definition—States which had them—Omnipotence of parliament, and municipal character of colonial governments—Difference in governments of Massachusetts, Connecticut, and Rhode Island . . . . 1—11

CHAPTER II.

AMERICAN CONFEDERATIONS FROM 1643-1790.

First confederation of New England (1643)—Object, nature, and effect of—Assumed the functions of an independent government—Treaty with France (1644)—Proposed one with the Governor of Canada (1648)—Population (1660) and (1760)—General Congress in New York of ten States (1765)—Declaration of rights—This first general government springs directly from the people, and not from the government of States—Lasted till 1781—Succeeded by the confederated government—Continental congress—Second congress from all the States in 1775—Delegates: how chosen—Troops to be raised—Money—General government—Nature of the confederation—Dr. Franklin's articles (1775), ratified, adopted (1786), nature of, defects . . . . . 12—17.

CHAPTER III.

COLONIAL GOVERNMENTS, ANCIENT AND MODERN.

Nature of first charters and character of colonists—Parliament no control of—Virtually independent—Established representative governments—Repealed common and statute laws—Repudiated Acts of Parliament passed expressly to bind them—Authority of King Charles's commissioners disputed—Charters not surrendered—Attempt to transplant Church and State—Rhode Island and Connecticut: nature of their governments—Self-made, well-governed communities—Contrast with

European—Functions of State and central government—Pure democracy—Growing into representative government—Is there sufficient power in central government?—Self-government in Europe a failure—State governments in America—Greek and Tyrian colonies in Asia, Africa, and Europe—Their nature—Carthage: its colonies—Commercial monopoly—Good government—Problem of colonial government—Should be left free, not trained for freedom—Roman colonies—Military posts—Governors—Origin of English and Grecian colonies—Character of colonization by military nations of modern Europe in contrast with early Mediterranean—Portugal and Spain—Division of the world by Pope Alexander VI.—Rise and fall of Portuguese power—Of Spanish—Of Dutch republic—The French —First representative government in America—Maryland, first province of the empire: its laws not subject to control of the Crown—Two houses—Titles of dignity—Disputes with Crown—Loss of charters—Rights claimed by Parliament—Charters granted to colonies by reformed Parliament, under William and Mary, less liberal—Extraordinary powers of governors—Right of taxation claimed by Parliament (1754) —Navigation Acts, 1651 and 1763—Powers of—Colonists before 1763 and after—Cause of change of feelings—Dr. Franklin's testimony in 1766—Growth of the States and their relations to England . . . . . . 18—35

CHAPTER IV.

INTRODUCTION OF PARLIAMENTARY OR RESPONSIBLE GOVERNMENTS.

British provinces in North America: their settlement, acquisition, government, &c.—Responsible government in Canada, struggle for—Edmund Burke—English statesmen: their policy—Lord John Russell's despatch (1839) on responsible government—Adderley's comments on—Style of argument in

Russell's despatch—Interference with internal policy of colonies inconsistent with despatch of Lord Glenelg (1839)—Disallowance of colonial Acts—Parliament would not legislate for colonies, nor allow colonies to legislate for themselves—New Brunswick — Bounties—Differential duties—Canadian tariff—Tormenting policy—Responsible government conceded to Canada (1846)—To maritime provinces from 1847-52—To Australia in 1856—Simple yet powerful remedy for colonial discontents: its effect . . . . 36—46

CHAPTER V.

CONFEDERATION OF BRITISH NORTH AMERICA.

Confederation of North American provinces (1864)—Meetings at Charlottetown and Quebec—Articles of confederation—Constitution of United States departed far from English model—British America returns to it—Difference between the two—Based on different principles—Power in central arm—Appointment of officers—Executive officers of the two governments—Errors of American republics—Evidences of compromises in articles of British American confederation—Central and local government — Local mostly municipal — Triple governments—Divided allegiance—Interests: local, federal, and imperial—Legislative council—Objections to its appointment—Its imperfections—Power of Crown to disallow—Composition of both houses—Lower Canada the pivot . 47—55

CHAPTER VI.

POLICY OF THE MOTHER COUNTRY.

Lessons taught in colonial history—Blunder in government of old colonies: its effect—No rigid rule in colonial government—Each colony must be treated on its own merits—Differ widely—Their population, Anglo-Saxon or mixed, dangers to each—England responsible for foreign relations of colonies—No British colony conquered—Have done their duty—None involved England in war—Rely chiefly on themselves—Will England go to war on any colonial question?—Fears her commerce and cost of war more than loss of colonies—Does America threaten England because Canada is English?—Conduct of America towards England and France—Of Germany towards same—Character of colonial populations: skilful riflemen, horsemen—Unlike the great mass of Europeans . . 56—60

CHAPTER VII.

COMMERCIAL POLICY.

Navigation Acts of 1651 and 1763: origin of—Rigorously enforced—Effect—Right to tax colonies: discussions of, in Parliament: Chatham: Grenville: Mansfield—Of nine millions of Englishmen (in 1763), eight not represented—Twelve millions in Great Britain not represented—Modification of navigation laws in 1824—Vacillating policy: effect on Canada (1843 and 1844)—Free trade: how far adopted in England: in India—British goods taxed by British freetraders—What was adopted in India denied to New Brunswick and opposed in Canada—Protection in Australia—Inconsistencies of the Colonial Office—the Secretary's opinions—Earl Grey—The theories of the minister of the hour forced upon the colonies—Differential duties—New Brunswick and the Colonial Office—Right of Parliament to legislate for colonies—Lord Glenelg's despatch: its violation—Is free trade the policy of the empire?—Revenue raised on imports: four millions on corn—Two-thirds of revenue on imports, &c., only one-sixth by direct taxation—Indirect taxes easily raised: direct, uncertain: lead to fraud: limited, and hard to collect—Mr. Laing—English free trade—English practice, not their theory, adopted in colonies—Foreign produce pays £24,000,000 at British ports before it can be admitted to British markets—Is this free trade?—£41,500,000 income collected on principles at variance with free trade—England free trade in theory only—Free trade and the Exchequer—Free trade and empire—Financial Association and Mr. Gladstone—The theory good, but the Chancellor cannot adopt it—Mr. Gladstone's principles applied to colonies—Necessities of their exchequers—Advantages—Public debt of Canada incurred in works that facilitate British trade—Mr. Gladstone's confession—English practice—Complaints by English freetraders of the working of this theory—Small revenue from direct taxes—Corruption, &c.—Free trade a policy, not a truth—Protection in colonies—Importance of manufactures to colonies—Price: markets—Increased population—Commerce —England as an agricultural country—What manufactures and commerce add—Importance of establishing manufactories in new countries—Example of old colonies—Southern States with ports blockaded . . . . . 61—88

CHAPTER VIII.

COST, DEFENCE, AND ADVANTAGES OF COLONIES.

Report of select committee of House of Commons for colonial expenditure for 1860—Two classes of colonies—Classification imperfect—Expenditure for each—Appropriations from colonies—Defence of British commerce, and not of colonies, object of British navy—Vast trade with colonies in comparison with cost—Australia—Canada—Expenses of navy, if no colonies, in peace, in war—Earl Grey—British America as part of the empire—Independent—Can it be conquered?—Campaign must be in summer only—Inaccessible fastnesses—Hardy population: trained to use of arms, &c.—Population and wealth—Proofs of loyalty—Civil and military expenditure: erroneous opinions—The Cape and New Zealand: what the

facts prove—Native affairs under Imperial government—
Foreign relations—Duke of Newcastle—Mr. Merivale—Archdeacons of Canada—Contrast between old and new colonies—
United States most aggressive power of the age—Canada: its
importance to the empire—Colonies would form other alliances
if cast off by England—Involved in Imperial policy—What are
the advantages to colonies?—To Mother Country?—Profits of
trade enormous—Chatham—A century of profits—Field for
emigration—Advantages of to England—Population and
means of subsistence—Capital and labour—Emigration to
United States: to Canada: to Australia—Imports from United
States and colonies: difference per person: profits—Trade of
Britain for 1863: greatest with colonies—British manufactures
to colonies: to United States—Defence of commerce—Trade
increased by colonial relation— Dr. Franklin—Trade of Britain
in 1704, and of colonies in 1861-3—Debate in House of Commons on Defences of Canada . . . . 89—128

CHAPTER IX.

OPINIONS, IMPERIAL AND COLONIAL.

I. Is it interest that binds colonies to the parent State?—Position of Canada and England reversed. II. Does England draw
the colonies, or the colonies England, into war?—English and
French policy as a peace policy—United States towards England and France—Mr. Adderley—Earl Grey—The Cape—New
Zealand. III. Institutions, ecclesiastical and civil, of old countries and new. IV. Canada during the civil war in America—
Mr. Adderley—Harsh and hasty opinions—Foreign policy—
Influence on Canada of a confederation on its border free from
slavery—England's relations to slave-holding countries—Duke
of Newcastle. V. Colonial systems—Past and present—Mr.
Adderley's reviewer—English writers on high spirit and international duties—Gladstone. VI. Cost of Colonies—Trade in

comparison with cost—Troops—Newcastle—Grey—New Zealand—Cape—Archdeacons and clergy reserves of Canada. VII. Old colonies—Policy of English statesmen. VIII. Imperial interests, how represented in colonies; and colonial in Mother Country. IX. Policy recommended by Committee of 1861—Godley—Merivale—Policy suggested by circumstances—No rigid rule—Newcastle—Grey. X. Mr. Adderley's contrast between old and new colonies—Virginia—Canada—Attributes acts of old colonies to wrong motives—Old colonies feared Parliament and Crown; and England the too rapid growth of colonies . . . . . 129—165

CHAPTER X.

EVIDENCE GIVEN BEFORE THE SELECT COMMITTEE OF THE HOUSE OF COMMONS ON COLONIAL MILITARY EXPENDITURE IN 1861.

Evidence before select committee, 1861—Duke of Newcastle—Mr. Merivale—Lord Herbert—General Burgoyne—Mr. Gladstone—Earl Grey—Mr. Godley—Mr. Brodie—Mr. Elliot—Mr. Lowe . . . . . . 166—194

CHAPTER XI.

FUTURE OF THE COLONIES.

Colonies as allies—Britain and her supremacy of the seas—Rapid growth of navies of France, Russia, and United States—The Colonies as maritime powers—Their strength added to that of England—Colonies and the strength of the empire—The 'Trent' affair—Attitude of Canada: Earl Derby on—What saved the nation from war—Lord Dufferin on the 'Trent,' and Canadian loyalty—Can the great branches of the Anglo-Saxon family be consolidated into one empire?—If not, is it the fault of the members or of the head?—The great colonies—Old colonies

—Present attitude of—Relation of old colonies to parent State—Parliament and the old colonies—Virtually independent and loyal—Only relations possible between England and those great dependencies—Common allegiance to the Throne—Legislatures of each—Independent, to what extent—Franchise in England: its extension—Effect of—Universal suffrage or greatly extended franchise in England—In the colonies—Great majority of voters in colonies owners of farms—Reverse in England—Policy of the empire—Who dictates it—New confederation of British America—Extent and resources—Population—Area of tillable soil compared with United States—Field for surplus population of England: its position: trade: tonnage: third among nations—Revenue—Surplus—Australia—Rapid development—Present position: population: trade: revenue, &c.—Independence of colonies—Their internal policy—Relations to England—Ships, colonies, and commerce—Colonies the foster-mothers of commerce—Earl Grey and Earl Derby on importance of colonies to the empire—Relations between Mother Country and colonies . . 195—225

APPENDIX.

Articles of Confederation of British North America—Dispatches of Governor General of Canada and of Colonial Secretary—Constitution of United States—Classification of colonies—Number of troops in each: infantry, Imperial and colonial, artillery, engineers—Imperial expenditure—Population, imports, exports, revenue, debt, duties, &c., of colonies—Names of colonies—Date and mode of acquisition—Population—Imports and exports per head of population of colonies compared with United States—Emigration from United Kingdom to colonies and to United States from 1815-64—Secretaries of State for colonies from 1768-1864 . . . 229—263

INDEX . . . . 265—271

AUTHORITIES.

Parliamentary Debates, Reports, Estimates, Returns, especially from 1760 to 1775, and during the last thirty years.

Reports of Colonial Legislatures.

Colonial Policy, Earl Grey. 1852. 2 vols.

Report of Committee of House of Commons, 1857, printed in 1859.

Report of Select Com. of the House of Commons on Colonial Military Expenditure. 1861.

Arthur Mills, M.P.—Colonial Constitutions. 1856.

Charters of Old English Colonies in America, by Samuel Lucas.

Story on Constitution of United States. 2 vols.

Graham's History of United States. 4 vols.

Bancroft's History. 8 vols.

Herman Merivale's Lectures on Colonization and Colonies. 1861.

Holmes' Annals. 1829.

Chalmers' Political Annals.

Right Hon. C. B. Adderley, M.P.—Pamphlet on Colonies. 1862.

Hallam, May, Russell, on Constitutional History of England.

Lord Brougham's Colonial Policy.

Flanigan's History of New South Wales.

BRITAIN AND HER COLONIES.

CHAPTER I.

GOVERNMENT OF THE FIRST ENGLISH COLONIES.

First Permanent English Settlement in America—The Two Centres of Colonization—Difference in their Origin and Development—First Representative Body—New England—Origin and Character of Government: Assemblies, Church, Oath of Supremacy, Pure Democracy, Representative Government—Charter by William and Mary, 1691—Blackstone's Divisions of Colonies—Omnipotence of Parliament—Pp. 1-11.

THE first permanent English settlement made in America was in 1606 under a charter from James I. to Sir Thomas Gates and his associates. That charter granted to them the territories in America lying on the sea-coast between the 34th and 45th degrees of north latitude, and the islands adjacent within 100 miles. The associates were divided into two companies, one was to settle between the 34th and 41st degrees of north latitude, and the other to the north. By degrees the name of Virginia was given to the first or southern colony; the second assumed the name of the Plymouth Company, and New England was founded by them.

The charter of the Virginia colony was altered in 1609 and 1612. From this period the progress of the two provinces, Virginia and New England, forms a regular and connected history. The former in the south and the latter in the north, may be considered as the original and parent states of the northern and southern portions of the republic. From these two centres, the one in Virginia and the other on Plymouth rock, have sprung two great groups of nations, differing in the character of their founders, in the development which the two have received, and destined apparently to diverge still more widely from each other in the future. The settlements in Virginia were the earliest by a few years. As they increased in numbers they grew impatient for the privileges which they had enjoyed under the government of their native country. To quiet this uneasiness, Sir George Yeardley, then the governor, called a general assembly, composed of the representatives of the various plantations. This assembly, which met at

James Town, in Virginia, in June 1619, composed of the governor, the newly-appointed council, and the delegates of the boroughs, constituted the first representative body convened in America. The general assembly was 'to imitate and follow the policy and form of government, laws, customs, and manner of trial used in the realm of England, as near as may be.'

In 1621 they received a written constitution. The form of government was analogous to that of England, and was, with some modifications, the model of the constitutions which were afterwards granted by the crown to the various colonies in America: a governor was to be appointed by the company; a permanent council likewise appointed by the company; a general assembly, to be convened yearly, to consist of the council and two burgesses to be chosen from each of the several plantations. The courts of justice were required to conform to the laws and manner of trial used in England. This corporation was dissolved in 1624, and the King issued a commission appointing a governor and twelve councillors, to whom was committed the government of the infant commonwealth.

The first settlers of New England, while yet at sea, drew up and signed an original compact, in which, after acknowledging themselves subjects of the crown of England, they declare, 'We covenant and combine ourselves together into a civil body politic for our better ordering and preservation; and by virtue hereof, do enact, constitute, and frame such just and equal laws and ordinances, acts, constitutions, and offices, from time to time, as shall be thought most meet and convenient for the general good of the colony.' This compact was signed by forty-one persons. It established a pure democracy. They organized a government under the name of New Plymouth, but considered themselves as planting a colony in the northern part of Virginia. They at once appointed a governor and other officers, and proceeded to enact laws. The governor was chosen annually by the freemen. The supreme legislative power resided in and was exercised by the whole body of the male inhabitants who were members of the church. A House of Representatives was established in 1639, the members of which, as well as all the other officers, were annually chosen.

The Plymouth colonists acted at first under the mutual agreement formed at sea. In 1629 a patent was obtained from the council at Plymouth, England, under the charter of James, given in 1620; but the patent not being confirmed by the crown, the colony remained in law a mere voluntary association. They did not fail, however, to avail themselves of all the provisions granted in that document. Having lost their charter in 1684, they were incorporated into a province with Massachusetts, under the charter to the latter by William and Mary in 1691.

In 1620 James I. granted to the Duke of Lennox and others of the Plymouth Company a new charter, extending its territories, and calling it New England. They were empowered to make laws, regulate trade, to appoint and remove governors and other officers, to establish all manner of orders, laws, &c., so that the same be not contrary to the laws of England. All the territory was to be holden of the crown, as of the royal manor of East Greenwich, of Hampton Court, or of Windsor Castle.

The Puritans procured, in 1627, from the council at Plymouth, a grant of all that part of New England indefinitely described as extending from the Atlantic to the South Sea. In 1628 King Charles granted to the grantees and their associates a charter with the most ample powers of government. The territory was to be holden of the crown, 'in free and common socage, and not in capite, nor by knight's service.' The grantees were called a body politic under the name of the Governor and Company of Massachusetts Bay, in New England, with the usual powers of corporations. The government was to be administered by a governor, a deputy governor, and eighteen associates, elected out of the freemen of the company. A court or quorum, consisting of the governor, or his deputy, and seven or more assistants, were to meet as often as once a month for the transaction of business. Four general assemblies, composed of the governor, deputy, assistants and freemen, were to be held every year, to admit others to the freedom of the company, elect officers, and make laws, &c., only 'such laws and ordinances must not be contrary to the laws and statutes of this our realm of England.' Every year at the Easter term, the governor, deputy, and other officers, were to be chosen. All subjects of the crown, and their children born there, or on the high seas going or returning, should enjoy all liberties and immunities of free and natural subjects, as if they were born within the realm of England. Many other provisions were added, similar in substance to those in the colonial charters previously granted.

The absence from this document of any clause providing for the free exercise of religion or the rights of conscience, is remarkable, considering the object of the Puritans in seeking a settlement in America, and in obtaining a charter from the king. These bold adventurers, however, paid no attention to this omission, but made their first church independent of the Church of England, and repudiated any connection with episcopacy or a liturgy. The oath of supremacy was to be administered to prevent the settlement there of Roman Catholics. The whole structure of the charter presupposes the residence of the company in England; but in August 1629, the government and patent were removed to New England. This infused new life into the colony, and it grew with such rapidity as to give it an ascendency amongst the New England settlements, and to awaken even the jealousy and vigilance of the parent state. The subsequent struggle between the crown and colony, down to the overthrow of the charter, under the famous *quo warranto* proceedings in 1684, manifested a disposition on the part of the colonists to yield nothing, and on the part of the crown to force them into subjection.

For three or four years after the removal of the charter all the business of the government was transacted by the freemen assembled in a general court. But the members having increased, so as to make a general assembly inconvenient for such purposes, an alteration was effected in 1634, and representatives were chosen, two from every town, to a general court. This general court was to have the sole power to make laws, to elect certain officers, to raise money and taxes, and sell lands. The great officers and magistrates were still to be chosen by an assembly of freemen. This change, not provided for in the charter, established the second house of representatives (the first being in Virginia) in the American colonies. The whole of the representatives and assistants sat in one house till 1644, when they were divided into two independent bodies.

From 1684 until 1691, the colonists were without a charter, the first one having been dissolved in the former year. In 1691 a charter was granted under William and Mary with new and enlarged powers, which continued down to the revolution in 1775. This embraced the old colony of Massachusetts Bay, New Plymouth, the province of Maine, Acadia or Nova Scotia, and all the lands between Nova Scotia and Mainé, and incorporated the whole under the name of the province of Massachusetts Bay in New England. It reserved to the crown the appointment of governor, lieutenant governor, the secretary of the province, and all the officers of the court of admiralty. Twenty-eight councillors were to be chosen annually by the general court, the governor and councillors were to have the power of directing the affairs of the province, and of appointing the judges, sheriffs, justices of the peace, &c. The governor was invested with the command of the militia. He had a negative also upon all laws passed by the general court. This court was to assemble annually, and to consist of the governor and council and the representatives of the towns, two from each; such representatives to be freeholders and annually elected by freeholders possessing a freehold of 40*s.* annual value, or other estate of the value of £40. The general court could change the number of representatives from each town. All laws were to be sent to England for approbation or disallowance. 'Liberty of conscience in the worship of God was allowed to all Christians, except Papists.' This charter the colonists hailed with sincere satisfaction, after the dangers which had for so long a time menaced their liberties and their peace.

Mr. Justice Blackstone divides the colonies into three classes—provincial, proprietary, and charter governments. The constitution of the first—the *provincial*—depended on the commissions issued by the crown to the governors. These commissions usually appointed a governor as the king's representative; the crown also appointed a council, who, besides the legislative authority, were to assist the governor in the discharge of his official duties. The commissions also contained authority to convene a general assembly of representatives of freeholders and planters, the council forming the upper, and the assembly the lower house. The governor, with the advice of his council, established courts, appointed judges, &c. Appeal lay to the king in council from the decisions of the courts. New Hampshire, New

York, Virginia, the Carolinas, and Georgia, had this form of government, some of them for a long time, and from an early period of their settlement.

Of the *proprietary* governments there were three only—Maryland, Pennsylvania, and Delaware. These were granted by the crown to individuals in the nature of feudatory principalities, with all the inferior royalties and subordinate powers of legislation which formerly belonged to the owners of counties palatine. The governors were appointed by the proprietaries, and legislative assemblies were convened under their authority. In Maryland its laws were not even subject to the supervision of the crown.

The *charter* governments Blackstone describes as ' in the nature of civil corporations, with the power of making bye-laws for their own internal regulations not contrary to the laws of England, and with such rights and authorities as are specially given them in their several charters of incorporation. They have a governor, named by the king, who is his representative or deputy. They have courts of justice of their own. Their general assemblies make laws suited to their own emergencies.' The parliament * of Great

---

* 'The colonies and plantations in America are subordinate unto and dependent upon the Imperial Crown and Parliament of Great Britain; and the King, with the advice and consent of Parliament, hath full power and authority to make laws and statutes to bind the colonies and people of America in all cases whatsoever.' (6 Geo. III. c. 12.)

Britain being in theory omnipotent, no doubt these colonial governments are merely municipal, whatever powers of legislation they may assume, and however complete under the crown and parliament their political organization may be. The only charter governments existing at the period of the American Revolution were those of Massachusetts, Rhode Island, and Connecticut.

The first charter of Massachusetts seemed to contemplate only a civil corporation within the realm, but the colonists exercised executive, legislative, and judicial powers upon the renewal of their charter. That of William and Mary, granted in 1691, was framed upon a broader foundation, and gave the usual powers contained in provincial charters. The governor was appointed by the crown; the council was chosen by the general assembly; and the house of representatives by the people. But in Connecticut and Rhode Island the charter governments were organized upon popular and democratic principles; the governor, council, and assembly being annually chosen by the freemen of the colony, and all other officers appointed by their authority.

CHAPTER II.

AMERICAN CONFEDERATIONS FROM 1643–1790.

Confederations from 1643 to 1790—Declaration of Rights—Character of the Confederations—Pp. 12-18.

As early as 1643, the New England colonies were united under a confederation. In 1637, less than twenty years after the first settlements, the subject had been discussed, and outlines of a union 'for offence and defence, material advice and assistance,' were drawn up. In May 1643, articles were signed at Boston between Massachusetts, Connecticut, New Haven, and Plymouth. The reasons assigned for this union were, the dispersed state of the colonies, the vicinity of the Dutch, Swiss, and French, the hostile disposition of the Indians, the appearance of a general combination of the savage tribes to exterminate the English, the commencement of civil contests in the parent state, and the impossibility of obtaining assistance from England in any emergency. They assumed the title of the United Colonies of New England. Immediately after its formation, several

Indian tribes sent in their submission to the new confederacy. This union, their historians inform us, rendered the colonies formidable to the Dutch and French as well as to the Indians, maintained general harmony among themselves, preserved them during the civil wars of England, contributed chiefly to their defence against the Indian King Philip, and was essentially serviceable in civilizing and Christianising the Indians. We find the United Colonies assuming at once the functions of an independent state, by entering the next year, 1644, into a treaty of peace with the French Governor of Acadia, proposing, in 1648, to D'Ailleboust, Governor of Canada, a similar treaty, and in 1652 preparing for hostilities apprehended on the part of the Dutch.*

In consequence of the dissatisfaction arising out of the Sugar Act of 1764 and the Stamp Act of 1765, Massachusetts proposed a general congress, to be held in New York. This congress, consisting of twenty-eight delegates from ten States, met at New York in October 1765. In their Declaration of Rights they set forth that they are entitled to all the rights and

---

* The population of all the colonies in America is estimated a few years later, 1660, at 80,000 (*Holmes' Ann.* p. 315); and in 1763, at about 1,500,000, Massachusetts alone having 240,000, and Pennsylvania 280,000; Canada only 100,000.

liberties of natural born subjects, amongst the most essential of which are the exclusive power to tax themselves, and the privilege of trial by jury. The grievance chiefly complained of was the Act granting certain Stamp Duties and other duties in the British colonies, which they declared to have a direct tendency to subvert their rights and liberties. A petition to the king and memorial to each house of parliament were agreed upon. The assemblies of Virginia, North Carolina, and Georgia, being prevented by their governors from sending representatives to the congress, forwarded petitions direct to England, similar to those adopted by that body. The following year, 1776, parliament repealed the Stamp Act.

The colonies having failed to obtain redress for their other grievances by appeals to the king and parliament, Massachusetts recommended, in 1774, the assembling of a continental congress. The delegates appointed, some by the legislatures and some by conventions of the people, met at Philadelphia in September 1774. The congress thus assembled exercised *de facto* and *de jure* a sovereign authority, not as delegated agents of the governments of the several colonies, but in virtue of original powers derived from the people. This, the first general or national government over the American States, sprang directly from the people, and not from the governments of the several colonies. It lasted till regularly superseded by the confederated government under the articles finally ratified in 1781. They adopted a declaration of rights, similar to that of the congress of 1765, affirming that the colonies are entitled to the common law of England, and to the benefit of such English statutes as existed at the time of their colonization. They signed articles containing an agreement of 'non-importation, non-exportation, and non-consumption,' in order to carry into effect the preceding resolves, and also an agreement to discontinue the slave trade.

In May 1775, a second congress of delegates met from all the states. These were chosen as the preceding had been, partly by the popular branch of the state legislatures when in session, but principally by conventions of the people. Amongst other acts, they authorised the raising of continental troops, the issuing of two millions of dollars in bills of credit, prohibited the receipt and registration of British government bills, framed rules for the government of the army, erected a general post-office, recommended Massachusetts to consider the offices of governor and lieutenant-governor vacant, authorised the equipment of armed vessels to intercept supplies to the British, and passed other such acts pointing to separation from the mother country, and evincing a determination at all hazards to maintain their rights. (Story's *Com.* i. 141.)

1. None of the colonies pretended to be independent States.

2. The colonies did not severally act for themselves, and proclaim their independence.

3. The power of the congresses to act was not derived from the State governments.

Dr. Franklin, in July 1775, submitted to congress a sketch of articles of confederation. In June 1776, the committee for preparing the Declaration of Independence was appointed, and another to propose the form of confederation to be entered into between the colonies. In 1778 the articles of confederation were ratified by all the States except Delaware and Maryland—by Delaware in 1779, and by Maryland in 1781, and adopted by the thirteen States in 1781.

The chief articles of the confederation were— 1. That the name should be the United States of America; 2. That each State should retain its sovereignty; 3. That the States severally entered into a league of friendship; 4. That the free inhabitants of each State should be entitled to all the privileges of free citizens in the several States; the fifth points out the manner of organizing congress, that the delegates should be chosen as each State directs; and the remaining articles give power to congress to determine on peace and war, to form treaties and alliances, to decide differences between two or more States, to regulate the value of coin, establish post-offices, and make laws relating to trade. This confederation, however well adapted to the exigencies of the times, fell to pieces from its imperfections, upon the restoration of peace. It gave no power to raise a revenue, to levy a tax, to enforce any law, to regulate trade, or to pay its own ministers at foreign courts. 'The United States by this compact may make treaties, but can only recommend their observance; they may appoint ambassadors, but cannot pay them; they may borrow money, but cannot pay a dollar; they may coin money, but cannot buy an ounce of bullion; they may make war, but cannot raise a single soldier. In short, they may declare everything, but do nothing.' (*Am. Mus.* 1786, p. 270.)

The Constitution—the new government of the United States—which took the place of the confederation, was finally adopted by all the States, in May 1790, Rhode Island being the last to assent to it. (*See* APPENDIX B.)

CHAPTER III.

COLONIAL GOVERNMENTS, ANCIENT AND MODERN.

First Charters—Powers Claimed—Repudiated Acts of Parliament—Disputed Authority of King's Commissioners—Self-made Governments—Greeks and Tyrians—Modern Colonizations—Self-Government in Europe—Colonial Governments of European States. Pp. 18-35.

THE charters granted to the first settlers in North America, in the beginning of the 17th century, were peculiarly adapted to the circumstances and characters of those bold pioneers of English colonization. The Stuarts regarded those colonies as parts of their own domain, and not as subject to the authority of Parliament; hence, when the House of Commons attempted to pass a law for establishing fisheries on the coasts of Virginia and New England, they were told by the Ministers of the Crown 'that this Bill was not proper for this House, as it concerneth America—it was not fit to make laws for those countries not annexed.' The charters contemplated the establishing of commercial companies rather than the founding of new States. The Crown claimed them as 'part of our manor of East Greenwich, of our Castle of Windsor, or of Hampton Court.' While thus free from the control of Parliament, they could annually elect and remove their governors and other officers; their general assemblies, also elected, could 'make and repeal such laws as to them shall seem meet, so as such laws shall not be contrary unto but agreeable to the laws of England,' raise an army, make war, 'invade and destroy the natives, Indians, or other enemies.'

Clothed with such powers, the colonists gave themselves little concern about King or Parliament in establishing such a polity as would suit them, 'considering,' in the words of their charter, 'the nature and constitution of the place and people.'

They assumed the liberty to dispense with such provisions of the charters as were found unsuitable to their position; and even to establish representative governments, when these were not, and it was seldom that they were, granted in express terms.

They carried with them the conviction that they were shorn of none of the rights of Englishmen by leaving their native land, but that they had freed themselves from many unnecessary restrictions, and that they breathed a freer air and enjoyed a more enlightened practical liberty.

'Notwithstanding the cautious reference,' says Judge Story, 'in the charters to the laws of England, the assemblies exercised the authority to abrogate every part of the common law,.except that which united the colonies to the parent State by the general ties of allegiance and dependency; and every part of the statute law except those Acts of Parliament which expressly prescribed rules for the colonies.' In the same spirit the New England colonies entered into a federal union in 1643, and into a treaty with France in 1644.

Massachusetts would not admit that the navigation laws were binding on her unless sanctioned by her own Legislature; and they remained a dead letter from 1651 to 1763. The Commissioners sent by King Charles II., in 1664, to demand the surrender of their charter, and forced, from the reception they received, to ask—'Did they (Mass.) acknowledge the authority of the King's Commissioners?' could get but this reply. 'The Court desired to be excused from giving any other answer than that they acknowledged the authority of His Majesty's charter, with which they were much better acquainted.' They also refused, in 1683, to be consenting parties to its abrogation, and only submitted to the decision of the King's Bench, which, on a *quo warranto*, ordered it to be cancelled; Connecticut, too, to save hers a few years later (1687), concealed it in the hollow of an old oak. The charters were to these bold and ardent puritans what the ark, with the tables of the law, was to the children of Israel. England, like Spain, wished to reproduce herself, —Church and State—in her dependencies. In 1642 the Church of England was established by law in Virginia, and in the Carolinas in 1704, about forty years after their settlement. 'It was specially ordered that no minister should preach or teach, publicly or privately, in Virginia, except in conformity to the constitution of the Church of England. Nonconformists were banished from the colony.' (*Bancroft*, i. 222.) The Act of Parliament of 1791 (31 Geo. III.), erecting Canada into two provinces, also established the Church of England in those colonies.

The provisions of the charters granted in 1628 to Massachusetts, and in 1662 to Rhode Island and Connecticut, were nearly the same, the chief differences being that liberty of conscience was expressly conceded to the inhabitants of Rhode Island, and they were not required to take the oaths of allegiance and supremacy; in the Connecticut charter no reference is made to religious matters. The colony of Rhode Island, founded by Roger Williams in 1636, was governed without a charter till 1662.

Driven from Massachusetts because he 'taught doctrines that seemed about to subvert the fundamental state and country,' Williams, after being 'sorely tossed in the wilderness for fourteen weeks,' landed, in a frail bark canoe, with five companions, at Providence, 'so called from his confidence in the providence of God.' Connecticut was settled the same year by Hooker and 100 of his congregation from Boston. They carried with them a commission from the Government of Massachusetts for the administration of justice in their new colony, but finding it beyond the jurisdiction of Massachusetts, formed themselves into a body politic, and continued thus to discharge all the functions of government until 1662, when they obtained a charter from King Charles II.

These colonies are fair examples of many similar ones throughout North America, which have grown into flourishing and well governed States from the smallest communities. They were at first voluntary associations. Connecticut and Rhode Island governed themselves for twenty-eight years without charters or constitutions. They were twigs broken off from the parent stock—Massachusetts, itself just planted. More than two centuries have elapsed since the founding of those infant States, and we find them at this day 'exhibiting,' as an able English writer says, 'the most successful polity on which the eye of the statesman can rest.' (*Merivale's Lectures*, p. 661.) How many dynasties have been subverted; how many constitutions, made for their own subjects or imposed on conquered provinces by kings themselves ignorant of constitutional liberty; how many people, struggling for a freedom but imperfectly understood, have perished in the attempt; yet these self-imposed constitutions, the most simple in their origin and the most natural in their growth, have stood the test of ages, happily blending, in those flourishing and vigorous communities, full protection to life and property with ample freedom. Nor can the deplorable civil war between the two great divisions of the republic be quoted as proof against the good government of individual states. The Federal Government has a written constitution empowering it to act for the whole in their relation to foreign states and to each other. Excepting the rights thus ceded, each state legislature is as absolute as the parliament of Great Britain; and we have the testimony of history to the truth of the statement that for more than two centuries have the older of these communities lived happily under the protection of a government established by themselves. 'To train the colonies for freedom,' is the language of English statesmen even at the present day; give them self-government at the very origin of their existence as separate communities, is the teaching of history. Rhode Island with but six citizens, and Connecticut with one hundred, governed themselves from their foundation. Their charters, when given twenty-eight years afterwards, served chiefly to mark their boundaries and guide their external relations, leaving their internal polity to themselves, or giving expression to what was already the outlines of a Constitution. In Massachusetts, too, the government was of the utmost simplicity in its origin. The governor was chosen by universal suffrage; his power was at first subordinate to the general will, but afterwards restricted by a council of five, and then of seven, assistants. For nearly twenty years the whole body of the male inhabitants of twenty-one years of age constituted the legislature, and the people were frequently convened to decide on executive and judicial questions. The increase of population and its diffusion over a wider territory led to the introduction, in 1639, of the representative system, and each town sent its committee to the general court.

In this cradle were rocked the infant constitutions of the new world. First purely democratic, the whole population being assembled to decide every question, then, when numbers and the extent of occupied territory rendered this no longer possible, representation was substituted. But still the democratic principle was retained through every department of State. It may be a problem yet to be solved, whether, with the increase of population, with large commercial and manufacturing centres, and with the multiplied and conflicting interests that must ensue, there will be strength in such governments to secure to their subjects the necessary protection. In the past they have served every purpose. For two and a half centuries there have been no revolutions against those State governments, no discontent; life and property have been secure. Little can be said, even at this day, in favour of self-government on the continent of Europe. It is there but an experiment in the last half of the nineteenth century; in North America, beginning with small communities of Englishmen, it has proved a success uninterruptedly from early in the seventeenth century. The earliest colonization on the shores of the Mediterranean teaches the same lesson. The history of some of those settlements comes to us, it is true, in but faint outlines from the eleventh and twelfth centuries before the Christian era; but enough is certain to show that they were independent communities from their origin. The English puritans in the seventeenth century knew no 'art of colonization' but that of taking care of themselves; the Greeks and Tyrians had done the same 3,000 years before. The Æolians from

Peloponnesus founded twelve cities in Lesser Asia; the Dorians sent colonies to Italy and Sicily. These speedily rivalled and even surpassed in prosperity the parent States. Carthage is reported to have been founded, seventy years before Rome, by a colony of Tyrians; and Tyre herself 240 years before the building of the temple of Jerusalem (1252 B. C.) by a colony of Sidonians, and indeed is called by Isaiah 'the daughter of Sidon.' In language, laws, and national character Carthage resembled Tyre. This renowned African city became in turn the mother country of numerous dependencies, and the centre of a vast dominion extending along a seaboard of 2,000 miles, over the chief islands in the western part of the Mediterranean, and on the coasts of Spain and even of Great Britain. For seven centuries she held 300 African cities tributary. Her colonial policy was a strict commercial monopoly. Her government, originally monarchical, like Tyre its parent, became at a very early period republican, in which aristocracy was a prevailing element. Its constitution was celebrated by Aristotle as one held in the greatest esteem by the ancients. From its foundation, he tells us, to his own time, upwards of 500 years, no considerable sedition had disturbed the peace, nor any tyrant oppressed the liberty of that State.

These were the most successful instances of colonization amongst the ancients, and they will lend us the best aid of any we can refer to in the solution of that problem which has so sorely vexed the statesmen of modern Europe—the government of colonies. They teach us the doctrine of *laissez faire* in reference to those vigorous offshoots from the parent stem. Left to themselves, they have a natural and healthy development. They are not 'squeezed' into preternatural shapes, nor do bandages stop their growth, as is the wont with the flat-head Indians and Chinese dames. 'To train them for freedom.' Somehow, we have got the notion that the moment a man leaves these shores a bit must be put into his mouth. If Lord Palmerston, burdened with the wisdom of eighty years, and with fifty of office, now confidently entrusted with the government of an empire on which the sun never sets, were to go abroad and become premier in the smallest of Britain's fifty colonies, the Parliament he has so long led would bridle and saddle him. If the whole Parliament were to migrate, the next one that takes its place would put these now renowned legislators under tutors and governors, 'to train them for freedom.'

To ancient Rome we turn in vain for any light on this difficult question. She enlarged her empire as modern Russia, as Austria, as Prussia, as Britain in India—by conquest. During the three centuries from Augustus to Diocletian, Roman colonization was simply the establishment of military posts, occupied by veterans, for State purposes. Of these we have an illustration in our own Imperial garrisons. From the first attempts to plant colonies in America to the last in British Columbia and Vancouvers, a period of three hundred years, our colonies have sprung, like those of ancient Greece, from discontent, from individual enterprise, or from commercial speculation. They have not been free from the control of the parent State to the same extent as, judging from the scanty annals left us of their foundation, were those of Phœnicia and Greece; but, compared with the colonies of other nations of modern Europe, our own in their early history have been subject to little restraint, their 'generous natures having been suffered to take their own way to perfection.'

The lessons to be learned from the results of the colonial policy of the nations of modern Europe are those of warning rather than of guidance.

We find little to please or encourage us in studying their history. What has been lost and what retained of those once vast empires are now but beacon lights on every continent and in every sea, to warn of fatal errors committed. The States which peopled the shores and islands of the Mediterranean and the coast of Europe were but *cities* with only municipal governments. The adventurers who went from these were from the first independent, and established governments similar to those of the parent State, adapting them to their altered circumstances. The maritime nations of Europe, the colonizers of modern times, are vast *military powers*, seeking the enlargement of their empires or the establishment of a commercial monopoly. In the pursuit of these objects they have sought the centralization in the mother country of all possible power over their dependencies. Pope Alexander VI. divided the world between Portugal and Spain. The East had been allotted to the former, and before the close of the fifteenth century she had planted numerous posts and colonies on both the East and West coasts of Africa, in Arabia, Persia, Hindostan, and the Eastern Archipelago, and later in Brazil. Her rigorous system of monopoly, the despotism of the sovereign, and the power of the priesthood, precipitated the downfall of Portuguese power. 'And now,' says Mills (p. 28), 'when the Azores and Madeira, Angola, and Mozambique, with an Indian and Chinese factory, and a few African slave depôts, complete the colonial roll of Portugal, it is difficult to realise the fact that there was an age when less than 40,000 armed Portuguese kept the whole coast of the ocean in awe, from China to

Morocco, when 150 sovereigns paid tribute to Lisbon.'

Spain received the West as the portion of the patrimony given her by the Roman Pontiff, who assumed the power to divide the earth between his two faithful children. Such a field for colonization as the two continents of the New World presented had never before been found. Spain, like Portugal, tried to transplant herself, State and Church, in her dependencies. Her hierarchy, her cloisters, and her inquisition, were incorporated with the civil power, and all dependent on the king. Thus a colonial policy, clearly defined and intimately interwoven with the parent State, had been established early in the sixteenth century. The colonial empire of Spain embraced most of South and Central America, Mexico, the West Indies, and Florida, and continued for 200 years. Now all that remains of these once vast foreign dominions are Cuba and Porto Rico, in the West Indies; the Philippines (which Spain, obedient to the injunctions of the Holy See, reached by going west); and a few unimportant settlements in Africa.

After the decline of Portugal and Spain from the high position of powerful maritime nations, Holland succeeded them as the chief carrier of the commerce of the world, and before the close of the seventeenth century numbered amongst her colonies Ceylon, the Cape of Good Hope, Guiana, several islands of the Antilles, five distinct governments under a trading company in the Indian Archipelago, and factories on the Coromandel and Malabar coasts, and in China and Japan. The Dutch Republic, at first the advocate of maritime freedom, followed the policy of the age, and centred in herself the trade and government of her colonies.

Surinam, Curacoa, St. Eustatius and settlements in Sumatra, Java and Molucca, are now all that remain of this once extended colonial empire.

The colonies of France embraced, a century ago, half the continent of North America; and in the East, Mauritius, Bourbon, and portions of the coast of India. Now she holds no part of North America, only Guiana and Cayenne in South America, Martinique and Guadaloupe, and some of the smaller of the Antilles in the West Indies, Bourbon and a fortress in Hindostan, and a depôt in Madagascar in the East, the Society Islands and New Caledonia in the Pacific, and Algiers—the last two named recent acquisitions.

The first representative legislature established in America, as stated above, was in Virginia. Sir George Yeardley had been appointed governor by the Company in 1619, and he promptly signified his intention of convoking a provincial assembly, framed with all possible analogy to the Parliament of the parent State. The first assembly consisted of the governor, the council, and a number of burgesses, who met in Jamestown, and 'discussed all matters that concerned the general welfare with good sense, moderation, and harmony.' 'But Maryland,' says Chalmers, 'has always enjoyed the unrivalled honour of being the first colony which was erected into a province of the English empire, governed regularly by laws enacted in a provincial legislature; nor were its laws made subject to the supremacy and control of the Crown.' In 1650 the burgesses were formed into a Lower House, and those called to the assembly by the special writ of the proprietary into the Upper House, thus establishing a miniature parliament. This charter, granted in 1632, empowered the proprietary to confer titles of dignity, to create manors and court barons, and the right of advowsons according to the Church of England.

While poor the colonists were left in the enjoyment of liberties conferred or assumed, with more or less tormenting from Crown and Parliament. Their disputes with the proprietaries or Crown led to the charters of the leading colonies being cancelled, and in passing from under the direct authority of the Crown to the Parliament they lost much of that freedom of action which had made them virtually independent commonwealths.

The new charter given to Massachusetts in 1691 by William and Mary was much less liberal in its provisions than that of Charles I. in 1628, and differed widely from the spirit even of those granted to the southern provinces. Under the first charter Massachusetts elected annually her governor and other officers; under the second, the appointment of all these functionaries was reserved to the Crown; to the governor was given a negative on the Acts of the assembly and council; all such Acts, too, were required to be sent to England for the royal approbation, and if disallowed within three years were to become void. Virginia was the centre and parent of the Southern as Massachusetts was of the Northern States. The first of her three charters was granted in 1606 to the London Company; in the second, in 1609, the local council was abolished, and the company dissolved in 1624. But the provincial assembly remained; yet the most extraordinary powers were conferred on the governors appointed by the Crown. 'He was,' says Bancroft (vol. iii. p. 20), 'at once lieutenant-general and admiral, lord treasurer and chancellor, the chief judge of all the courts, president of the council, and bishop or ordinary; so that the armed force, the revenue, the interpretation of the law, the administration of justice, the church,—all were under his control.'

In 1754 Parliament claimed the right to tax the colonies. The Navigation Act had been passed in 1651, but was a dead letter until 1763, when Grenville obtained a new one, and enforced it on all the American sea-board with more than Spanish rigour. The Act gave authority 'to employ the ships, seamen and officers of the navy as custom-house officers and informers.' The Stamp Act was also proposed in this year (1763) by the Secretary of the Treasury, and passed in 1765.

When Dr. Franklin was examined before the House of Commons in January 1766, to the question, 'What was the temper of America before 1763?' he replied, 'The best in the world. They were led by a thread. They had not only a respect, but an affection for Great Britain, for its people, its laws, its customs, and manners; and even a fondness for its fashions that greatly increased the commerce.' 'And what is their temper now?' (1766) — 'Oh, very much changed. They considered Parliament the great bulwark and security of their liberties, and always spoke of it with the utmost respect and veneration.' 'And have they not the same respect for Parliament now?'—'No; it is greatly lessened.' 'To what cause is this owing?'—'To restraints lately laid on their trade; the prohibition of making paper money among themselves, and then demanding a new and heavy tax by stamps, taking away at the same time trial by jury.' To the question, 'Suppose Great Britain should be at war in Europe, would North America contribute to the support of it?' Dr. Franklin answered, 'I think they would. They consider themselves as part of the British Empire, and as having one common interest with it.'

How unwise and how stern must have been that policy which could turn allies so faithful as they had proved themselves into the most implacable enemies! These thirteen colonies have grown into thirty-three independent states, and those less than three millions of British subjects into thirty-three millions of foreigners, who have been enemies of Britain, but never allies; whose moral influence in peace or war the land of their fathers never feels. Whatever may be said of the cause of that revolution, or of the continued want of amity towards Britain on the part of her American descendants, this, at all events, cannot be denied, that England failed to retain the allegiance of those most loyal and vigorous communities of her own race while under the British Crown, and to secure their friendship after their separation from it. These are of that class of blunders, seeds sown in the infancy of society, the bitter fruits of which do not mature till the far off future, till it may be the old age of the nation.

CHAPTER IV.

INTRODUCTION OF PARLIAMENTARY OR RESPONSIBLE GOVERNMENTS.

British America—Responsible Government—Its Effects—Burke—Colonial Office—Disputes—Colonial Tariffs. Pp. 36-46.

To the north of the Great Republic, in the magnificent valley of the St. Lawrence, have grown up other British communities once the possessions of a foreign Power, whilst those that were British, from their foundation, are now foreign. A wiser policy has made these flourishing provinces, in 1863, what Dr. Franklin described the old ones to have been a century before, in 1763, 'British in feeling—considering themselves as part of the British Empire, and as having one common interest with it.'

Newfoundland had been occupied by the English as early as Virginia (1608). Nova Scotia, discovered by Cabot of Bristol, in 1497, came finally into the possession of Britain in 1713, after having been alternately under the French and English. New

Brunswick, like Upper Canada, was settled by the United Empire Loyalists in 1783, after the close of the American revolution; and, in 1784, separated from Nova Scotia, of which she had previously formed a part.

Quebec was captured by Wolfe in 1759, and Canada ceded to Britain at the treaty of Paris, in 1763. It was erected into a province in 1784, and divided into Upper and Lower Canada in 1791, and again united, fifty years afterwards, in 1841. Representative institutions were granted in 1791, a governor and legislative council appointed by the Crown, and an assembly elected by the people. The Act of 1841, uniting again the two provinces, enlarged the powers of their legislature. Canada had asked for a government based upon the same principles as the British constitution—the responsibility of the advisers of the Crown to Parliament. The resolutions of the Canadian House of Assembly, passed in September 1841, clearly express the nature of their demand.

1. 'That the head of the executive government of the province, being within the limits of his government the representative of the sovereign, is responsible to the Imperial authority alone; but that, nevertheless, the management of our local affairs can only be conducted by him, by and with

the assistance, counsel, and information of subordinate officers in the province.'.

2. 'That the chief advisers of the representative of the sovereign, constituting a provincial administration under him, ought to be men possessed of the confidence of the representatives of the people.'

Responsible government was made the test question at the elections in the maritime provinces, as well as in Canada; but British statesmen in this, as in many other instances, so long turned a deaf ear to just demands, that when the concessions came they were received without thanks, because yielded without grace. The colonists called to mind the contrast between their condition and that of the first settlers in America; that those acting under charters from the arbitrary Stuarts had really more freedom of action, both in their internal affairs and external relations during the first half of the seventeenth, than they in the middle of the nineteenth century; but the statesmen of England seemed to have forgotten that the attempts to restrain that liberty produced the angry dissensions ending in the loss of those colonies; and that in the spirit of their government they differed little from their ancestors of three generations before. There were indeed men at that day who enunciated in substance the principles of colonial government since adopted with such happy results. Foremost among these was Edmund Burke, who, with that extraordinary insight into human affairs, and that practical wisdom drawn from history, which so distinguished him, used these remarkable words, in 1775, in moving his 'Resolutions for conciliation with America':—

'My hold of the colonies is in the close affection which grows from common names, from kindred blood, from similar privileges and equal protection. These are ties which, though light as air, are as strong as iron. Let the colonies always keep the idea of their civil rights associated with your government, they will cling and grapple to you, and no power under Heaven will be able to tear them from your allegiance. But let it once be understood that your government may be one thing and their privileges another, the cement is gone, the cohesion is loosened, and everything hastens to decay and dissolution. As long as you have the wisdom to keep the sovereign authority of this country as the sanctuary of liberty, the sacred temple consecrated to our common faith, wherever the chosen race and sons of England worship freedom, they will turn their faces towards you. The more they multiply, the more friends you will have; the more ardently they love liberty, the more perfect will be their obedience.'

In contrast with these noble and generous sentiments, so true and so beautifully expressed, are the opinions of the British Cabinet, as given by the Colonial Minister in 1839. Through the entire struggle for constitutional government, there was exhibited, on the one hand, the moderation of the colonists, and their thorough knowledge of their necessities; on the other, the tenacity with which English statesmen cling to their hereditary policy, and their inability, apparently, to comprehend the condition and wants of communities constituted so unlike their own. In a despatch, addressed to Lord Sydenham, the Governor-General of the North American provinces, October 14, 1839, Lord John Russell, in a style of argument peculiarly his own, by which the ever-changing questions of policy are solved with mathematical exactness, demonstrated that a system of government similar to that of England is impossible in a colony, and inconsistent with its relation to the mother country.

'You may,' he says, 'have to encounter much difficulty in subduing the excitement on the question of "responsible government." I have to instruct you, however, to *refuse* any explanation which may be construed to imply an acquiescence in the petitions and addresses upon that subject. If the governor is to obey his instructions from England, the parallel of constitutional responsibility entirely fails; if he is to follow the advice of his council, he is no longer a subordinate officer, but an independent sovereign. The power for which a minister is responsible in England is not his own power, but the power of the Crown, of which he is the organ. It is obvious that the executive councillor of a colony is in a situation totally different. The governor under whom he serves receives his orders from the Crown of England. But the colonial officers cannot be the advisers of the Crown of England. It may happen that the governor receives, at the same time, instructions from the Queen and advice from his council totally at variance. It would have been impossible for any minister to support in Parliament the measures which a ministry, headed by M. Papineau, would have imposed on the governor of Lower Canada.'

'Lord John's difficulty,' says Mr. Adderley, 'was based on the supposition that colonial legislation must in all things be made subservient to the will of the English Parliament—the old rock again on which American connection split.' The governor was to be made an instrument of torture to show those distant British communities that 'their privileges were one thing, and the Crown another.'

If such opinions had continued to influence the advisers of the Crown, no doubt can exist in the minds of any who knew the state of public feeling in those provinces that they would have demanded the right to elect their own governors, since Lord Russell had made the position of that officer appointed by the Crown an insuperable objection to ceding responsible government. The first colonists had elected their own governors and all the subordinate officers; they had in that state continued most prosperous and loyal, and it was not till after the appointment by the Crown of governors to look after Imperial interests that disaffection was ever breathed. Lord John Russell created in 1848-50 and 1851 the very supposititious case which he had proposed in 1839 as a test of the practical working of responsible government by 'giving instructions to colonial governors totally at variance with the advice which they had received from their own council.' His government fell back upon the omnipotence of Parliament to legislate for every part of the empire, and from behind this impregnable fortress announced to the Lieutenant-Governor of New Brunswick, that 'in adopting the policy of free trade Parliament did not abdicate the duty and power of regulating the commercial policy not only of the United Kingdom, but of the British Empire,' on the broad and generous principles that 'the common interest of all parts of that extended empire requires that its commercial policy should be the same throughout its numerous dependencies.' No one of those dependencies, however, had ever asked for the establishment of this policy, but all that have expressed any opinions upon it have virtually rejected it. The government of New Brunswick had passed an Act in 1848, granting bounties on the cultivation of hemp, but Lord John Russell's ministry advised its disallowance, as at variance with the new-born commercial policy of the minister of the day. Yet the right of legislating on all internal questions had been conceded in 1839 in Lord Glenelg's despatch to Sir Francis Bond Head; but here the Imperial Parliament would neither legislate herself nor permit the colony to legislate on a purely local matter. So also in the dispute between the Home authorities and New Brunswick, that province was not allowed to impose differential duties on imports from the United States. Again, the advisers of the Crown interfered in the recent rearrangement of the Canadian tariff for purely revenue purposes, and with a like result. But responsible government is being more firmly established by these ordeals. It is quite impossible that a people, who have created their wealth out of the wilderness, and made a nation with all its multiplied interests, can understand the justice or the wisdom of another nation overriding their legislation and dictating in their local and vital affairs. Let the British Parliament but ask themselves what would be their indignation if another authority, or another people, or even any power within the nation, could, after dictating and sketching the outlines of measures, and influencing their legislation, lay their hand upon any statute passed within the last two or three years and annul it, and that this was sometimes done; they may then form some conception of the opinions entertained by British subjects in those distant provinces of the tormenting policy to which at times they are subjected.

Responsible government was however conceded to Canada in 1846, and to the other North American provinces under the colonial administration of Earl Grey, between 1847 and 1852; and some four years later, in 1856, to the Australian colonies.* The instituting of this change, so simple in its nature, requiring but the consent—a despatch—of the Home

---

* By the Acts of Parliament of 1842 and 1850, the legislatures of the Australian colonies were made to consist of a single chamber, of which one-third of the members were nominated by the Crown. Legislatures have now been created with two chambers—none of the members of which are nominated. The suffrage is a manhood suffrage, and vote by ballot. In the North American colonies, the legislatures were composed of two houses, but the franchise is restricted very much the same as in England, and the question of the introduction of the ballot has never been even much discussed. In Canada, both chambers are elected.

Government, and yet so powerful in its effects upon the whole machinery of the government in those provinces where it was introduced, removed at once every ground of complaint against the parent state. The appointment to places of power and emolument before made by the governor on his sole authority, or acting under instructions from the ministers of the Crown; responsibility for the entire policy of the government, whether relating to its measures in the legislature or to its purely executive acts; all such powers within the limits of a subordinate legislature as pertain by usage to the ministry in England, passed with this 'transcript of the British constitution' into the hands of the administration, the privy council of the colony. That council is appointed by the Crown as before, but is responsible to the House of Assembly, the House of Commons of the province.

Mr. Merivale, who expresses himself with so much good sense and generous feeling on the relation of Britain to her dependencies, has these appropriate remarks upon the introduction of responsible government into the colonies :

'The magnitude of that change—the extraordinary rapidity of its beneficial effects—it is scarcely possible to exaggerate. None but those who have traced it can recognise the sudden spring made by a young community under its first release from the old tie of subjection, moderate as that tie really was. The cessation, as if by magic, of old irritant sores between colony and mother country is the first result. Not only are they at an end, but they seem to leave hardly any trace in the public mind behind them. Confidence and affection towards the 'Home,' still fondly so termed by the colonist as well as the emigrant, seem to supersede at once distrust and hostility. Loyalty, which was before the badge of a class suspected by the rest of the community, became the common watch-word of all; and with some extravagance in its sentiment, there arises no small share of its nobleness and devotion. Communities which but a few years ago would have wrangled over the smallest items of public expenditure to which they were invited by the executive to contribute, have vied with each other in their subscriptions to purposes of British interest, in response to calls on humanity or munificence, for objects but indistinctly heard of at the distance of half the world. Nor is the advance in social progress, contemporaneous with this change, less remarkable than the improvement in public feeling.' (*Lectures*, p. 642.)

CHAPTER V.

UNION OF BRITISH NORTH AMERICAN PROVINCES.

Confederation of North American Provinces—How it differs from the United States. Pp. 47-56.

ONE of the most important state papers of the age, certainly the most important connected with British North America, has just been published. This document embodies the result of the conference held at Quebec in October 1864, on the subject of a confederation of the British provinces in North America. For many years, and more especially during the last twelve or fifteen years, the question of a closer union between those colonies had been more or less discussed; but it had always been felt that public opinion was not sufficiently matured upon it to justify any immediate action. In September, an informal meeting was held at Charlottetown, Prince Edwards, by members of the governments of Canada, New Brunswick, Nova Scotia, and Prince Edwards, and a resolution, which received the support of all the delegates, was passed to the effect that a union between Canada and the maritime provinces was desirable. Representatives from these provinces were summoned by the Governor-General to meet at Quebec on the 11th of October, 1864. The results of that conference are set forth in the Articles of Union, given in Appendix A, and with them, for convenience of comparison, a summary of the constitution of the United States (Appendix B). The framers of the American constitution seem to have departed as far as possible from the pattern which was necessarily their guide—the government of Great Britain. The people of British America, on the other hand, living by the side of the Great Republic, and having from the beginning marked the working of the two systems, have laboured to mould their own institutions, as far as the changed circumstances would permit, after the model of the parent State. The statesmen of British America have wisely given expression to public opinion throughout those provinces in following the precedents set them by their forefathers under a government which has secured protection with enlightened freedom for so many ages. The theory that government is for the people and springs from the people, has been pushed in America to the extreme of electing not only their president, governors, and senators, but in many cases even their judges. Without calling in question this principle, lying at the base of the entire political system of their southern neighbours, and followed as their guiding star almost to the exclusion of every other element in good government, the infant States growing up in the great valley of the St. Lawrence, in seeking to lay broader the foundations of their national superstructure, ask for the appointment of all these officers by the Crown, the supreme head of the confederation. A viceroy, the nominee of the Crown, is to be Governor-General over all the united provinces. The Upper House, or Legislative Council of the central government, the judges, and the governors of each of these confederated provinces, are to be appointed by this viceroy, by the advice of his executive council. This council, unlike the ministers of the President at Washington, are members of Parliament and responsible to it; they are also legislative as well as executive officers, unlike the secretaries of the central government at Washington, who are only executive. The House of Assembly, too, may be dissolved by the Governor-General, thus allowing an immediate appeal to the country; the House of Representatives of the American Republic must run its appointed time.

The Republics of America in the northern and southern hemispheres, in dread of the despotisms springing from the too great concentration of power in many of the governments of the old world, have run a greater danger—that of anarchy. For fear of giving too much, they have given too little strength to the central arm. The revolutions and counter-revolutions of the Republics of that continent, are the result. Protection, without which government is a delusion, has been sacrificed to extravagant ideas of liberty. The young Republics of the North, for virtually they are republics, have sought for the older land-marks of the old world, and laboured to make protection the central idea of their political system.

Under the Crown of Great Britain there is to be a general government charged with matters of common interests to the whole, and local governments for each of the provinces—the Canadas, New Brunswick, Nova Scotia, and Prince Edwards—having the control of local affairs, provision being made for the admission into the Union of Newfoundland, the Northwest territory, British Columbia, and Vancouver. The general government is to follow the model of the British constitution as far as circumstances will permit.

In this carefully-drawn paper there are evidences of compromises between those who wished to preserve the sovereignty of each of the contracting commonwealths and those who would have placed the whole under one legislature. The inherent weakness and complicated machinery of confederacies and their history, even upon the American continent, could not but awaken in the minds of the framers of this constitution many misgivings as to its adaptation to the government of so many countries, with their diversified interests, extending over territories so vast. In the infancy of those communities there may be strength in the central government to meet all their wants; but it may be very different when these now young and vigorous States, each of which is capable of sustaining a population equal to many an European kingdom, shall have grown into powerful nations, with large commercial and manufacturing centres. All honour is due to those patriotic men who contended so strenuously for the sovereignty of their own provinces; but it may prove to have been zeal without knowledge. The very spirit which has led them, in the infancy of their organization, to be so jealous of local in opposition to general interests, will grow with their growth, and, as in the United States and Central and South America, sectional interests or State rights may become too strong for the Federal government. New York, Pennsylvania, Ohio, or Virginia, with populations of ten or twelve millions, which they are well capable of sustaining, would assume more and more the attitude of independent

States, and by consequence weaken their connection with the general government. The question of the sovereignty of each State has become one of vital importance in the American Republic, and has strengthened with the increase of population in each. The same tendency may be looked for in the British-American confederation. To guard against this, more power is reserved to the federal government, and less given to the local. In the American Union each State is assumed to be an independent nation, and the general government has only such powers as the States severally have ceded to it. In the new confederation the chief power is attempted to be centred in the general government, and only municipal functions given to the local governments.

Again, and intimately connected with this, are the questions growing out of the relations between the local and central legislatures, the divided allegiance, and in this case the triple allegiance, due to the local, federal, and imperial governments. Local interests, as against federal, are sure to increase the attachment, the patriotism, of the inhabitants of each State for their own province, and weaken it towards the confederation ; and confederate interests, as against imperial, must likewise create and strengthen a purely colonial party. This plurality of governments we conceive to be the weak point in the new constitution. The world, it has been said, is too much governed; but here are three governments over one and the same people. This was no doubt a necessity to some extent; for a confederation under the Crown of Great Britain was universally demanded by the loyal people of all those provinces; then local interests had to be considered. That, however, which many will think would have proved the wiser policy, would have been one parliament under the Crown for all the provinces, with only municipal powers conceded to the local. The present constitution is no doubt the result of compromises from the many interests concerned.

Art. XI. provides that the members of the Legislative Council are to be appointed by the Crown, under the great seal of the general government. That such a chamber, under any representative government, has little influence, is the universal experience. Even in England, with all the prestige that high titles and wealth and usage have given, the House of Peers has not maintained its ancient position. The popular assembly has monopolized the chief power and patronage in the State; and virtually Great Britain is a democracy under a restricted franchise, with one house elected every three or four, and at longest every seven years. As the House of Commons, in Canada as in England, is omnipotent *because elected*, one cannot but regret that the elective principle is not to be applied to the Upper House in the new confederation. None can deny the vast importance of securing men of large experience, who have successfully served the public, as members of the Lower House and as ministers of the Crown, as judges or ambassadors; yet, with all these to add to the hereditary peers in the House of Lords, that estate is waning in influence before the elected house; and a nominated chamber in a new country can hardly be expected to obtain, compared with the popular branch of the legislature, a status as good as the House of Peers in England. The number of legislative councillors, moreover, being fixed, leaves no provision for the inevitable dead-lock which must often occur between the two houses.

That every bill of the general parliament, as stated in the 50th Article, is to be subject to disallowance by the Sovereign within two years, as is now the case, gives a power which can only annoy the colonists, and subject them to humiliation if exercised; and if of no use, why should it be retained? It can do no good; it may work harm. 'It can be only mischievous,' said the Duke of Newcastle, in reference to the Imperial government keeping in their own hands the management of the natives of New Zealand, 'to retain a shadow of control where any beneficial exercise of it has become impossible.' The correctness of this opinion has received a too speedy corroboration in the Maori war, and especially in the disputes between the governor of that colony and his council, growing out of the control assumed over all native affairs by the governor, after his promise to take the advice of his council, and after the establishment of responsible or constitutional government.

The Upper House, or Legislative Council, is to be composed of representatives from three great divisions—Upper Canada, Lower Canada, and the maritime provinces—each of which is to send twenty-four members. The Lower House, or House of Commons, as it is called in the Articles of Union, is to be made up of representatives from each province in proportion to their population. Upper Canada to have 82 members, Lower Canada 65, New Brunswick 15, Nova Scotia 19, Prince Edward's 5, and Newfoundland 8. The census is to be taken every ten years, and the representatives from each province are to be readjusted on the basis of the then population. Lower Canada, continuing to have 65 members, is to be the pivot, as it were, on which the whole are to revolve. At every returning decennium the number of representatives from each province is, in the readjustment, to bear the same ratio to its population as 65 does to the then population of Lower Canada.

CHAPTER VI.

POLICY OF THE MOTHER COUNTRY.

Colonial Policy—Will England Defend her Colonies—Involves them in her Foreign Policy—Duty of the Colonists. Pp. 56–61.

THE colonial history of England, even thus briefly traced, throws much light upon the relations which should be maintained between the parent State and her dependencies. The first communities of Englishmen planted abroad were virtually independent, and at the same time truly loyal to the throne; by the interference of Crown and Parliament they were driven from their allegiance, became a powerful confederation of States, and have ever since shown a want of amity, not to say exhibited a positive hostility, towards the nation that gave them birth. The two great members of the Anglo-Saxon family have been enemies, but never allies. Other scions from the parent stem have taken root in foreign soil, and now supply the place of those goodly branches which have fallen off. These are so numerous, the field over which they are scattered so vast, and the elements of which they are composed so diversified, that it would be vain to expect to lay down any rigid system for their treatment. The practical statesman will deal with each on its own merits. The circumstances of the fifty colonies may differ as widely from each other as fifty independent States. Some of them are great communities of Englishmen, virtually independent nations, with complete self-government; others are made up of the untutored savages, simple children of nature, ignorant of nothing so much, in their profound ignorance, as of the civil polity and all that pertains to government amongst the more enlightened nations of Europe and America; others again, composed of Anglo-Saxons and Aborigines, are disturbed by such questions as naturally spring from the union, or attempted union, of races so widely differing from each other; and all by their peculiar dangers internally, or by their relations externally. The fortresses, naval and military stations, the trading and anti-slavery posts, form another class or other classes peculiar to themselves.

It would be monstrous to suppose that the British government would retain the absolute control over the foreign relations of every member of the empire, yet in war be responsible only for the defence of her own shores and firesides; and that she would involve the distant dependencies in her quarrels, it may be, against their will and their interests, and then leave them to their fate, bound hand and foot. This has never been English policy, and never can be until England ceases to be English.

That the colonies will always be ready to bear their part in the defences, not only of their own shores, but of the empire at large, their whole history abundantly proves. No British colony has ever yet been conquered; and when attacked through the policy of the mother country, they have had to rely chiefly on their own sons, although these largely go to recruit the army and navy of England. The colonies are in most danger when least assistance can be rendered them, as in the war in 1812–15, when every soldier and sailor and ship and sabre was engaged in the all-devouring peninsular and continental wars.

Nor has any policy or folly of the colonies ever involved the mother country in hostilities. They are drawn or driven by a power not their own in all their foreign relations. They may be the chief sufferers, their country may be the battlefield, and all because of their connection with the empire; but they have always manfully borne the part which has fallen to them. Since the 'Ashburton capitulation' no colonists believe that England will go to war on a purely colonial question. 'America would not have threatened us,' say English statesmen and writers, 'had not Canada been part of the empire.' 'England fears her commerce and the cost of war, and not the loss of Canada or danger to her,' is the retort of the colonist. Questions of trade and cost were as prominent in the threatened war with Germany as was the pretended fear for Canada in the apprehended imbroglio with America.

The colonies must rely on their Militia and Volunteers for defence. Standing armies with them must be their last resort, and spring from a terrible necessity. The efficiency of such forces for defence was proved in the war of 1812–15. The Militia of Canada then nobly defended her shores against vast odds. The history of the Southern Confederacy teaches a like lesson. In those new countries the youth grow up familiar with firearms. The rifle is their plaything. They are the best of horsemen, they are skilful with the oar, the axe, and the spade, and accustomed to all those manly out-door exercises which best qualify them for duties in war. They are, in all these matters, quite unlike the great mass of any European population.

The Volunteer force, while furnishing a most efficient arm for defence, is the least likely to involve their country in foreign wars. This is now the policy of Britain, and English statesmen would confer more benefit upon mankind by labouring to fashion the military establishments of Europe after this model than by attempting to reproduce in Canada the continental organization so productive of foreign wars and national bankruptcy. The Volunteer system, as a substitute for the present military organization in Europe, except for police purposes, if seriously proposed, would be pronounced a dream of the theorist; but if it existed at this time none would deny that it would be the first great step towards preventing international wars, and would be a vast saving to national exchequers, and, by releasing the capital and labour now absorbed in creating instruments of destruction, give a wonderful impetus to those industrial arts which contribute most to the wealth and material prosperity of nations.

CHAPTER VII.

COMMERCIAL POLICY.

Navigation Acts of 1651 and 1763: Origin and Effects of—Chatham, Grenville, and Mansfield on Rights of Parliament—Modification of Navigation Laws, 1824-43-46—Theory and Practice of Free-trade in England—India—Protection in the Colonies—Colonial Office—Vacillation—Violation of its own Dispatches—Free-trade not the Policy of the Empire—Duties on Corn—Revenue how raised: in India: in Colonies—Financial Association and Mr. Gladstone—His Confession—Revenue and Protection in Colonies—Manufactures in Colonies—Another Industry—Its Importance—Example of old Colonies—Southern Confederation—England, Agriculture, Manufactures and Commerce—Australia. Pp. 61-88.

In the middle of the seventeenth century the Dutch Republic had already monopolized the immense commerce which the daring enterprise of Spain and Portugal had opened to the maritime nations of Europe both in the Eastern and Western hemispheres. English merchants freighted the vessels of Holland with their own wares because of their lower rates, and even imported through them the products of English settlements, while their own vessels lay rotting in port. To secure the now important and rapidly increasing commerce, and to keep the colonies dependent on the parent state, Parliament enacted, in 1651—

'That no merchandise, either of Asia, Africa, or America, including also the English plantations there, should be imported into England in any but English-built ships, and belonging to England or English plantation subjects, navigated by English commanders, and three-fourths of the sailors to be English.'

The Commonwealth thus founded that restrictive commercial policy, the source of so many disputes between the parent State and her dependencies, and which, revived in 1763, was one of the chief causes of the American revolution of 1775. From their foundation the trade of the older colonies had been perfectly free, and continued much the same after the passing of this Act, for New England constantly evaded it. In 1763 Grenville obtained a new Act. Against the remonstrances of the colonists and the warning of many English statesmen, it was enforced with the utmost rigour on all the American coast. The Act gave authority to employ the ships, seamen, and officers of the Navy as Custom-house officers and informers. From the mouth of the St. Lawrence to Cape Florida every commander of an armed vessel had authority to stop and examine and, in case of suspicion, to seize any merchant ship approaching the colonies. Massachusetts, through her house of representatives, remonstrated against this, the Sugar and Stamp Acts, demanding their repeal, and protesting against the imposition of any taxes upon American colonies, on the ground that not being represented in the British Parliament they could not be taxed.

Dr. Franklin, who represented the American States in London, was examined before the House of Commons, in 1766, on the effect which these measures had produced in the minds of the colonists. 'They were most loyal before 1763. Now their temper was greatly altered, owing to restraints on their trade, the prohibition to make paper money, and the tax by stamps. They had previously regarded Parliament as the great bulwark of their liberties; but their respect for Parliament was now greatly lessened.'

The whole question of the right of Parliament to legislate for and tax the colonies was then fully discussed in the Lords and Commons. In both that right was affirmed; in the former with only four dissentients, and in the latter with not more than ten.

Lord Chatham sustained the view taken by the colonists. 'America,' he said, 'being neither really nor virtually represented at Westminster, cannot be held legally, nor constitutionally, nor reasonably, to obedience to any money bill of this kingdom. The Americans are the sons, not the bastards, of England.

As subjects they are entitled to the common rights of representation. Taxation is no part of the governing power. Parliament may legislate for the colonies, but taxes are a voluntary gift and grant of the Commons alone. The idea of the virtual representation of America in this House is the most contemptible that ever entered the head of man.'

'That this kingdom,' said Grenville, 'is the sovereign and supreme legislative power over America cannot be denied; and taxation is a part of that sovereign power. Great Britain protects America; America is bound to yield obedience. When they want the protection of this kingdom they are always ready to ask it. That protection has always been afforded them in the most full and ample manner. The nation has run itself into immense debt to give it them; and now that they are called upon to contribute a small share towards an expense arising from themselves, they renounce your authority and insult your officers.'

'I am charged,' replied Chatham, 'with giving birth to sedition in America. The gentleman tells us America is obstinate; America is in open rebellion. I rejoice that America has resisted. The profits to Great Britain from the trade of the colonies is two millions a year. This is the fund that carried you triumphantly through the last war. I dare not say how much higher these profits may be augmented.'

Mansfield carried the House of Lords with him against the remonstrances of the young American States. 'No one,' he said, ' would live long enough to see an end put to the mischief which will be the result of the doctrine that has been inculcated. The doctrine of representation seems ill-founded. There are 12,000,000 of people in England and Ireland who are not represented. The notion that every subject must be represented is purely ideal. There can be no doubt but that the inhabitants of the colonies are as much represented in Parliament as the greatest part of the people of England; amongst 9,000,000 of whom there are 8,000,000 who have no votes in electing members of Parliament. Proceed, my Lord, with spirit and firmness, and when you have established your authority, it will be time to show your leniency.'

The effect of the navigation laws was to concentrate the trade of the empire in the mother country, to restrict the markets of the colonies, and to reduce them to the greatest dependence upon Parliament— the very evil they had always dreaded and struggled against. 'High protection duties were imposed on the productions of foreign colonies, and bounties given; but British colonies were prohibited from carrying on various branches of manufactures, and foreign manufactured goods imported into the colonies were placed under the same duties to which they were liable in the mother country.' (*Merivale's Lectures*, p. 76.)

England had attained the foremost rank in commerce and manufactures under this restrictive policy. The navigation laws, so it was assumed, protected these interests. In 1824 they were modified; in 1843 another Act was passed favouring colonial produce; but in 1846 the present free-trade policy of the nation was initiated. Earl Grey has given us some illustrations of the mischievous effects upon the dependencies of the empire of the vacillation of the mother country on this vital question. 'By the Canada Corn Act of 1843, in consideration of a duty of 3s. a quarter having been imposed by the provincial Legislature on the importation of foreign wheat, not only the wheat of Canada, but also its flour, were admitted for consumption into this country. Much of the available capital of the province was laid out in making arrangements for manufacturing flour of American wheat, as well as of their own. But almost before these arrangements were fully completed, and the recently built mills fairly at work, the Act of 1846 swept away the advantages conferred, and thus brought upon the province a *frightful amount of loss* and a great derangement of the colonial finances.' (*Col. Pol.* i. 220.)

The commerce and manufactures of Britain could no longer suffer from competition. Her unrivalled mercantile marine, the position and nature of her manufactures, and her great wealth, rendered free-trade a necessity if she would reap the full advantages of her position.

She was sure to centre in herself the greatest portion of the commerce of the world. Her merchantmen would bring the raw material to her mills, and take the manufactured articles to every country of the globe.

Her ports would be the chief emporiums of trade for the commercial world.

Her coal, her iron, her cheap labour, and her very climate, free from great extremes of heat and cold, rendering possible that long sustained and continuous labour so essential in heavy manufactures, put at rest all questions of rivalry in her peculiar industrial arts. One has only to become familiar with the every-day routine of labour in the workshops of England and of other countries, to be convinced of the great advantages which the climate of these islands gives the manufacturer. It is not in the hot and sultry portions of the earth, but almost exclusively in the cooler regions of the temperate zones, that the heavy manufactures have established themselves. 'We cannot compete with you,' said a Frenchman at the International Exhibition of 1862, 'in the great manufactures of your country. Our people cannot sustain the hard and continuous labour necessary for them.' Yet with all these advantages Great Britain adopts free-trade only in name. She still taxes her commerce £24,000,000 a year for revenue purposes, and £24,000,000 is too much to pay for even this noble truth. Other nations were invited to reciprocate this freedom in trade. In the meantime India, with a fifth of the population of the globe, becomes a part of the empire, and presents a magnificent field for testing a theory so beautiful, and a truth so self-evident. But free-trade is found inconsistent with the interests of that vast country after being incorporated with Britain. English manufactures, free before, are taxed on their introduction into India by English statesmen, themselves free-traders. But that which has been adopted in India, was denied to New Brunswick, and opposed in Canada. In Australia, a continent of colonies, protection to colonial industry has become a popular cry of the candidates for popular favour. Protection, they say, may be good for an old country, but cannot be applied to a new one, while the old can undersell the new in all manufactures. The old country must have free-trade. Her cheap labour, her wealth, her commerce, demand it. Our boys, say the Australians, what shall we do with them? We have no occupation for them. India, the only country ruled directly by the Crown, has her coasts lined by a cordon of custom-houses, and that too by those who were in theory uncompromising free-traders.* (*Melbourne Cor. Times*, September 16, 1864.)

* Since writing the above, we have received the following account of the last elections in Victoria :—

'One of the three demands made of the candidates in the last election for Victoria, the most populous of the Australian colonies, was the revision of the tariff to secure as much protection to colonial manufactures as may be necessary in shifting our present import duties, in whole or in part, from tea, coffee, and sugar, to such English and foreign manufactures as we can produce in the colony. The elections are just over (October 25, 1864), and the candidates were elected on protection, and the minister (the Premier) has adopted this policy. During the elections, the Princess of Wales' ornaments were constantly referred to. They were manufactured in Melbourne. There were 17s. 6d. an ounce duties on them, which were only remitted in England out of consideration for Her Royal Highness. "If England," it is said, "still protects her industry against colonial industry, why should not the latter act in the same manner against England? Why should a custom claimed in these free-trade days good for England, be so very bad for a colony? Industry should be nursed at first. It cannot spring up without it. Our natural advantages will admit our successfully producing many things, if we can get a start: this is best effected by duties."' (*Melbourne Cor. Times*, December 14, 1864.)

Earl Grey informs us in his 'Colonial Policy' (i. 18) 'That the interference of the servants of the Crown in the internal affairs of the old colonies and the differences which that interference occasioned, arose almost entirely from the endeavour to uphold the commercial system then in force.' And again in the same letter, 'Much of the opposition we (Earl Russell's ministry, 1850-2), have met with, and the principal difficulties we have encountered, have arisen, directly or indirectly, from our having thought it our duty to maintain the policy of free-trade, and to extend its application to the produce of the colonies. The greatest service that I believed we were called upon as a government to render to the country, was securely establishing a system of free-trade throughout the empire' (i. 4 id.). From an expounder of the colonial policy of England, seeking to draw lessons of wisdom from the sad pages of the past, one would scarcely have expected to find, in the same letter, and almost on the same pages, the minister of the Crown asserting it to be his duty to maintain the now commercial system of the mother country, in the face of an opposition as wide-spread and conducted, as far as it has gone, in the same manner as that which, he informs us, led, in opposing the then commercial system, to such deplorable results three-quarters of a century before. Earl

Grey gives us a sample of the difficulties his government met with in endeavouring to render that greatest of services, by forcing all parts of the empire into a uniformity with the theories of the ministers of the hour. In his instructions to the Lieutenant-Governor of New Brunswick, requiring the free-trade policy of England to be adopted by the colonies, he gives this peculiarly English view, founded upon uncertain information, or possibly formed without any information at all, of the necessities of all those numerous dependencies of the empire :—

'When Parliament determined upon abandoning the former policy of endeavouring to promote the commerce of the empire by an artificial system of restriction, and upon adopting in its place the policy of free-trade, it *did not abdicate the duty and the power of regulating the commercial policy, not only of the United Kingdom, but of the British Empire.* The common interest of all parts of that extended empire requires that its commercial policy should be the same throughout its numerous dependencies' (i. 281).

After asking the withdrawal of these instructions, New Brunswick addressed to the British Government a minute of its executive council, intimating a strong wish that the legislature of the province should be allowed to impose differential duties on importations from the United States (p. 283). Earl Grey, the colonial minister, replied to this request, on November 1, 1850, that the 'British Government declined to withdraw or modify the instructions.' In April 28, 1851, 'The Assembly of New Brunswick voted some strong resolutions asserting its right to pass measures of the kind objected to' (p. 285). And Lord John Russell's ministry went out of office without withdrawing their instructions.

Mr. Mills gives an example to the same effect, but one which also illustrates another point. In 1839, the Secretary of State for the Colonies, Lord Glenelg, 'instructed' Sir Francis Bond Head, Lieutenant-Governor of Upper Canada, that—

'Parliamentary legislation on any subject of exclusively internal concern to any British colony, is, as a general rule, unconstitutional, and yet, when in 1848 the legislature of New Brunswick passed a law granting bounties on the cultivation of hemp, it was deemed constitutional to disallow that enactment, because it conflicted with the political bias of the executive government.' (*Mills' Col. Con.* p. 41.).

Theoretically, free-trade is assumed to be the policy of the nation, practically, it is nothing of the kind. England need not, and does not, attempt to foster her commerce or manufactures by any artificial means. She, however, raises annually £4,000,000 revenue by duty on corn, and a quarter of a million on timber (£272,000 in 1864, of which £188,390 were on Canadian timber), which protects, to this extent, her home produce. What do the colonies more by customs duties on imports, necessarily the chief source of revenue? Great Britain does not adopt free-trade either at home or in India. Call it indirect taxation or protection, she makes up two-thirds of her revenue by taxes on articles of consumption, by customs and excise, and not one-sixth by direct taxes, viz. the property-tax and assessed taxes.* Mr. Laing, who sums up his politics in the two words 'free-trade and non-intervention,' says of this system of raising the revenue, after his India experience:—

'It is a most simple, productive, and, in the main, equitable mode of raising the necessary revenue, and I believe that after the recent reforms and reductions which have been carried out by Mr. Gladstone, little more remains to be done in the way of adjustment of taxation.

'The greater substitution of direct for indirect

---

* England raises £23,000,000 by customs of her £67,000,000 revenue, Canada $6,000,000 by customs of her $15,000,000 revenue. In England the proportion by customs to the whole revenue is as 1 to 2·870, in Canada as 1 to 2·500, only a fraction in favour of free-trade England. In Australia the proportion by customs is still less.

taxation may be a favourite theme with theorists, but it will not stand the test of practice.

'Direct taxation is open to the fatal objection, that if uncertain, it leads to fraud and vexation, and, if limited to certain incomes and objects, it involves glaring inequality, by omitting others as real though not so easily ascertainable. A tax like the income-tax is only rendered tolerable, first, by being applied to a community sufficiently intelligent to appreciate its necessity; secondly, by being moderate in amount; thirdly, by being an habitual tax, not involving any great amount of inquisitorial inquiry. When these conditions are wanting, as I found them in India, an income-tax is the worst possible tax, from the excessive disproportion between the sum realised to the State and the annoyance and demoralization caused to the community. Compare this with the extreme ease with which large sums are levied by indirect taxation almost imperceptibly, or even, it may be, with positive advantage to the community. Some theorists have talked as if taxation on imports were inconsistent with free-trade; and Mr. Bright once broached a budget on this principle, in which he proposed an income-tax of half-a-crown in the pound as a substitute for customs. Free-trade has nothing to do with the question. It simply requires that import duties, like other taxes, should be levied simply and solely with a view to revenue. No doubt all taxes are evils. We endeavour to solve the problem by taxing pernicious luxuries, such as spirits, heavily; harmless luxuries, and articles of general consumption, not positively necessaries of life, moderately; and necessaries [corn, £4,000,000] and all raw materials of industry, not at all.'

If this be free-trade, then Earl Grey, who laboured so hard, and apparently to so little purpose, to force it upon the colonies, the Chancellor of the Exchequer, and the free-traders in and out of Parliament, who have made incessant and bitter complaints against the Canadian revenue laws, must now congratulate themselves upon having converted those noble provinces to the free-trade policy of the empire. Canada taxes imports; England does the same both at home and in India. Canada does not tax corn or timber, for she has a surplus; but England does, to the extent of four millions and a quarter a year. Canada taxes manufactured goods which she imports; England does not, for she exports them. Both tax tea, sugar, and coffee lightly; but alcoholic and other nervous stimulants heavily. Both admit raw materials free, but England taxes the most important necessary heavily, though Mr. Laing says she does not—the shilling on corn bringing into the revenue four millions a year. But 'free-trade has nothing to do with the question!'

It would be a misnomer to call this free-trade, or to say that trade is free, while shackled with such clogs. The revenue from customs alone is £24,000,000, and from customs and excise, £41,448,583. While foreign produce must pay £24,000,000 annually at British ports before it can be admitted to British markets, it is too soon to talk of free-trade being the policy of the empire. By throwing the duty off the raw material and reducing it on bread-stuffs, the British manufacturer must be benefited to this extent, and if foreign nations would, in return, admit British manufactures free, this country would, unquestionably, be highly benefited by the reciprocity. None question the wisdom of this policy for Britain.

Neither the Chancellor of the Exchequer nor any of the early and great expounders of free-trade, have taken such a narrow view of its principles. But statesmen who have the responsibility of providing for the public revenue, find that the necessities of State must limit the application of these theories. Revenue and empire seem both antagonistic to free-trade; in other words, free-trade, fully carried out, would ruin the British exchequer, and break up the British empire. We say nothing of free-trade in the abstract, if, abstractly, such a thing were a possibility.

If any believe that they can form in trade, or science, or morals, a theory independently of all facts, they will, at all events, admit that its value is to be found in practice.

However beautiful and noble the theory, none will deny that it has been found inconsistent with the exigencies of the State. So, too, we believe the rigid adoption of free-trade, as the policy of the empire, would be the adoption of an element of dissolution; it would be the introduction into the national system of a centrifugal force too powerful for the centripetal; the cohesion would be loosened, and the distant members of this vast and magnificent empire would fall off.

The Financial Association of Liverpool, in their address to Mr. Gladstone, the Chancellor of the Exchequer, October 13, 1864, state that he had acknowledged the duty on corn to be impolitic, and yet as to wheat had increased its amount; that the effect of this was undoubtedly to occasion a corresponding increase in the price of all homegrown produce; so that it was, in truth, a protection tax, amounting to some £4,000,000 annually, although we were supposed to have got entirely rid of protection. With really free-trade in the article, this country would speedily become the depôt for the world's surplus corn. It was, therefore, the Association complains, exceedingly to be regretted that, instead of taking a penny off the income-tax this year, that penny had not been retained, and the corn-tax abolished.

Mr. Gladstone, in his reply, after admitting that he had given his opinion in his place in Parliament that the tax which still remains on corn is a tax that in principle cannot be defended, makes a statement which ought to be remembered by himself and others when censuring the revenue laws of some of the colonies, namely, that a minister of the Crown must consider what measures will receive the support of Parliament.

"I am not able,' says Mr. Gladstone, ' to accept the doctrine that an error was committed, as the address says, by me, and I must of course say, in order to speak the truth, by the administration of the Queen, when we preferred to ask the House of Commons for the remission of a penny from the income-tax, rather than to take off the tax on corn. Now, the simple test to which I bring that question is this: Supposing we had not proposed to take a penny off the income-tax, but had proposed to remit the shilling on corn, during the last session of Parliament—because that is the whole question—the question of time and circumstances—will you guarantee to me that such a proposal made by Government would have had success? Direct taxation, I admit, if we were to proceed upon abstract principles, is a sound principle; but, gentlemen, have some compassion upon those whose first necessity, whose first duty, it is to provide for the maintenance of the public credit, to provide for defences of the country, to provide in every department for the full efficiency of the public service. I wish I could teach every political philosopher and every financial reformer to extend some indulgence to those who would ascend along with them, if they could, into the seventh heaven of speculation, but who have weights and clogs tied to their feet, which bind them down to earth. Let no government be induced under the notion of abstract, extensive, sudden, sweeping reforms, to endanger the vital principle of public credit or to risk throwing the finances of the country into confusion.'

Mr. Gladstone has, with others, found fault with the customs laws of Canada.* Why did he not first

---

* Mr. Gladstone in his speech on the budget of 1865 (see London papers, April 28, 1865) labours to prove that the malt-tax of seven millions and a half falls on the consumer; and the *Times* (April 29) says, 'Mr. Gladstone has *conclusively proved* that the malt-tax falls on the consumer, and not on the producer.' Why then are not Canadian duties, so much complained of, a tax on the consumer, and not on the English producer? Cotton and woollen goods are much more necessaries for the Canadian than apply here, as in his own case, his 'simple test,' whether his proposal—for, of course, as an experienced minister he had a substitute for that to which he so strongly objects—'would have had success?' Why did he not extend some indulgence to the Canadian Ministry, who might be willing 'to ascend along with him, if they could, to the seventh heaven of speculation, but who have weights and clogs which bind them down to earth?' Why would he not allow them the benefit of his sensible advice, 'that no government, under the notion of abstract reforms, should endanger the public credit, or risk throwing the finances of the country into confusion?' Canada had undertaken vast and expensive public works. Her customs duties are her chief source of revenue. What else could she do? Her canals and railways save more on the transit of English manufactures than the customs impose. Through Canadian canals, and over Canadian railways, British manufactures are now carried two thousand miles into the interior of the continent to regions they could never before reach. Canadian bread-stuffs, of which she has as

beer for the Englishman. The Canadian farmer who may have £10 for the purchase of cotton goods for his family would buy no more by first laying aside £1 for the income-tax, and then paying the £9 for his goods, than by paying the £10 direct for his fabrics; besides, the cost of the machinery for collecting the income-tax in new countries would absorb all the receipts.

great a surplus as all the United States, and timber, although heavy of transit, are now easily brought to the sea-ports at greatly reduced prices through the same channels. Thus, if it were a mere balancing of profit and loss between the tariff at Canadian sea-ports and the lower freights by means of her canals and railways, the English manufacturer would be greatly the gainer.

'Direct taxation,' says Mr. Gladstone, 'I admit, if we were to proceed upon abstract principles, is a *sound principle*, but,' etc.

This is an extraordinary apology coming from a free-trader. A theoretical principle, good in the abstract, especially for those who dwell in the seventh heaven of speculation, but have mercy on those who have anything to do with it in practice. Nor can we believe that the adoption or rejection of free-trade can be put on the ground Mr. Gladstone rests it on—the prejudices of Parliament—'the time and the circumstances'—to which he refers it. It simply proves that trade is not the only interest in the nation. But the free-trader will listen to none of these things. The exigencies of the exchequer, the existence of the army and navy, and may be the very existence of the government, the integrity of the empire, questions of foreign and domestic policy, every interest except commerce,—all may stand in uncompromising opposition to his interpretation of his theory; but he yields nothing; so much the worse for those mighty interests, *tant pis pour les faits*, if they oppose his theory.

Nor could Canada, if so disposed, adopt free-trade. She has undertaken gigantic works to facilitate her own traffic and that of foreign States passing through her country. On her canals, which admit vessels of 600 tons 1,200 miles from the ocean to the head of Lake Ontario, and of 400 tons to Lake Superior, a distance of 2,000 miles, she has expended $20,000,000, and an equal sum also on her 2,000 miles of railways: these, with that portion of the municipal debt, chiefly invested in railways, for which the government is responsible, make her debt for public works £10,000,000 sterling. Whence is a young country, thinly settled and with little accumulated wealth, to get the means of paying this debt? The municipalities, the towns, the cities, already tax themselves for their roads and bridges, which must be made *de novo*, and for other expenses peculiar to a new country. India and England, the oldest and richest of countries, with their accumulated wealth of centuries, cannot dispense with customs duties.

The 'Times,' which calls free-trade 'the noblest truth that has dawned on political science' (September 6, 1864), and condemns the colonies in no mild terms for not abolishing their custom-houses and relying on direct taxation for their revenue, puts in this strong plea for indirect against direct taxation (August 13, 1864) :—

'Before they (legacy and succession duties) acquire a lengthened prescription, may we venture to ask whether the annoyance they impose and the sort of bodily fear under which they put every man of property or in trust, are not to be an element in the question between direct and indirect taxation. There are those who point triumphantly to the larger produce of indirect over direct taxation, and rush to the conclusion that the poor are taxed more heavily than the rich. To this conclusion we demur, but if these people will be so good as to add that the indirect taxes are collected easily, and paid most readily, then they have completed the case in favour of indirect taxation over direct. You need never use an article unless you choose. As to trade and the immense commercial development which has followed reduced duties, we are glad of it, but we do not see why national prosperity is always to be set against individual comfort, or why any class is to be rendered miserable for the good of the State.'

On the 12th of August (1864), the same journal has these strictures on the political and moral effects of the income-tax :—

'The false returns [only 310,000 persons in Great Britain and Ireland in a population of 30,000,000 having been returned in 1863 as paying income-tax, and more than half these paying on under £150 a year] are, as a rule, made by the lesser merchants, professional men, and tradesmen—a class in fact having at present most interest at elections, and *whose opinions determine the policy of the nation.* There is no argument against the continuance of the income-tax so potent as the deterioration of political morality it begets in the lower classes. Politicians would be justified by this consideration in endeavouring to abolish it, were there any hope, which there is not, of achieving such a result.'*

If direct taxation in a State with the hoarded wealth of centuries, so easily reached by the tax-gatherer, wrings such language from those who

---

* Number of persons assessed in 1863 in Great Britain, 293,468; in Ireland, 17,000; total, 310,468, or one in a hundred.

Sixty-seven persons in Great Britain, and three in Ireland, were assessed at or above £50,000; 8,000 in Great Britain, and 400 in Ireland, from £600 to £1,000. More than one-half, say 160,000, pay on incomes below £150; 130,000 on incomes from £150 to £600; 8,470 on incomes above £1,000; 18,070 on incomes above £600. Incomes assessed in Great Britain at £93,322,864; in Ireland at £4,677,000; total, £97,999,864. The income-tax was imposed in 1842 for three years only; in 1845 was prolonged for three years more; in 1848 for three years again, then two years successively for twelve months only. In 1853, Mr. Gladstone registered a solemn vow that it should die in 1860.

ask for the universal application of free-trade, and would yield nothing to those who regard such questions of trade to be not a science but a policy* to be adapted to circumstances, a strong case is already

* That free-trade is regarded as a policy to be adopted or rejected according to the necessities or supposed necessities of communities, is well illustrated by the actions of the various Australian colonies in their trade regulations. In New Zealand and Tasmania, islands, each under one government, the revenue is made up chiefly by customs duties; and in New Zealand they have been lately increased. In South Australia also, the chief port being insulated and not capable of being used as an *entrepôt* of trade, with other parts of Australia, *ad valorem* duties have for some time been imposed. The case of New South Wales, again, is entirely different. The port of Sydney possesses a large trade with the interior, for most of which there is so sharp a competition with other ports that it has even lost a portion of its trade. Sydney also has a considerable coasting trade, to which the same remark applies. It was not necessary, therefore, to try the experiment of protection to see the consequences of it, although the government had for a few weeks enforced a protection tariff. Business men saw that it would involve diminished trade, and thereupon, without troubling themselves with abstract theories, came to the conclusion that protection was unsuited to New South Wales in its present state, and voted against it. The ministry, too, were unpopular, and this helped to defeat them. In Victoria, however, protection is as popular as free-trade is unpopular in its sister colony; yet a protectionist ministry held the reins of power for more than a year in even New South Wales. 'It is fortunate,' says the 'Sydney Herald,' 'that the protectionist scheme in Victoria was not launched till ours was disposed of. Had they established their protection tariff, pushed as we were for revenue, we would have been in greater danger of being drawn into it.'

made out in favour of customs duties in countries thinly settled and possessed of little wealth, where the expenses of collection would equal or even exceed the sums realized. But the question in Canada is not entirely between direct and indirect taxation. They seem not unwilling to give protection to certain manufactures so far as to encourage their establishment, but only to such as, being firmly rooted, would stand without any further assistance. They reason thus. We, they say, have the raw material, the wool and the flax for example. We now pay all the cost and charges on these to England and back; packing, carting, wharfage, insurance, freight, &c. both ways; we send the food to feed the manufacturers. Our products, as those of all agricultural countries, are of great bulk, and the expenses of transit enormous. If we can get the capital, the machinery, and skilled labour established in our own country, we shall save all the expenses just enumerated. We shall economize much labour in new fields of enterprise for those whose inclinations or habits better qualify them for manufactures and the arts which they foster, and for those, never an inconsiderable proportion of any people, who are incapable of profitable employment in any other pursuits. We shall add another population to the agricultural; we shall secure customers at our own doors in the numerous manufacturing communities in our midst for the products of our gardens and fields, now unsaleable. Protection will make us at first pay a higher price for these wares, but experience has proved that competition in our midst will bring down the price again. But even if it should not, we are compensated in the better markets for our products, in the lessening of our taxes by the increase in our population; one kind of manufactures will beget another, and these again others; commerce will multiply, and with commerce another population will be superadded. England, as a purely agricultural country, could not support more than 5,000,000 souls; her manufactures add another 5,000,000, and commerce another five. But another consideration, not very distinctly defined nor often expressed, is ever present in the minds of her statesmen and scholars. War may come, as it comes to all nations; few generations pass away without carrying with them sad memories of its devastation. War may come upon them in their weakness and in their infancy, and they may be shut out from all the world, as were the old thirteen colonies, and as are the new Confederate States, without the manufactures necessary for defence and for domestic purposes. Admitting the doctrine of the disciples of free-trade, that protection checks a nation's progress, how small an ill would this be in comparison with what the Southern States, and especially the old colonies, suffered when first they began their struggle for all that a people hold dear. In the midst of war with a great and warlike nation, and with their ports blockaded, they created their most necessary manufactures. While learning to make the cannon and the musket, the powder and the ball, they were training the men to use them; they were making at the same time an army and a navy, and laying the foundation for the most necessary manufactures.

CHAPTER VIII.

COST, DEFENCE, AND ADVANTAGES OF COLONIES.

Report of Select Committee of House of Commons on Colonial Expenditure, 1861—Classifications—Navy chiefly to Defend British Commerce—Expense would be greater if no Colonies—Military Posts—Vast Trade with Colonies with little Cost—British America: its Population, Defence—Erroneous Opinions on Expenditure—Foreign Relations of Colonies—Contrast between old and new—United States an Aggressive Power—Colonies if cast off—Mother Country and Colonies—Profits of Trade enormous—Fields for Surplus Population—Capital and Labour more Productive—Trade greatest with Colonies—Defences. Pp. 89-128.

THE Imperial expenditure for colonial military and naval purposes contained in the Report of Mr. Mills' Select Committee is that for 1860. The dependencies of the British empire are there divided into two classes :—

1. Those which it is stated may properly be called 'colonies,' the defence of which is undertaken mainly for their own protection, though they may in some instances contain within their boundaries posts held for Imperial purposes. To this class belong the

North American and South African colonies, the West Indies, the Eastern colonies of Ceylon, Mauritius and Labuan, as also New South Wales, Victoria, Queensland, South Australia, Tasmania, and New Zealand.

2. Those of which the defence is undertaken exclusively for Imperial purposes, whether as military or naval stations, convict depôts, or for other objects of Imperial policy. To this class belong the three Mediterranean dependencies, Malta, Gibraltar, and the Ionian Islands (since surrendered), Hong Kong, Bermuda, the Bahamas, St. Helena and the Falkland Islands, West Australia, and the three African settlements of Sierra Leone, Gambia, and the Gold Coast.

' In order to arrive at a fair estimate of the average annual expenditure incurred and of the number of troops employed, the Committee obtained returns for the year ending March 31, 1860, the most recent period during which no disturbing causes existed, involving an abnormal increase of force in foreign possessions.' (See Appendix.)

' Throughout their inquiries,' the Committee state that ' they have deemed it essential to keep in view the distinction to be drawn between these two classes.'

Ceylon, Mauritius, and Labuan, mostly with native populations, and the last with but two thousand souls, are grouped in the report with the great Australian colonies; and the West Indies with the North American, as all alike or 'mainly' defended for their own sake. 'Out of the £2,000,000,' says Mr. Merivale, 'for which the Imperial expenditure of 1858 for colonial military purposes was fairly reducible, £1,000,000 was expended in two colonies alone, the Cape of Good Hope and New Zealand, both at that time in profound peace with their savage inmates or neighbours.' Why should even these two colonies in their present condition be classed with those two great groups of provinces—the North American and Australian—none of which have ever drawn the mother country into war, or required her aid against internal foes? Canada has been twice involved in war with a powerful neighbour on solely Imperial questions, and on a policy now condemned by every English statesman, but in both instances defended herself with little assistance.

The Parliamentary Committee of 1861 place the Imperial expenditure for the first-class of colonies at £1,715,246, including under this head those to which exception has just been taken; and for the second-class, £1,509,835. Of the former sum, the appropriations for the first-class, £413,566 were expended in the four North American colonies, including Halifax, Quebec, and Kingston, the first at all events a most important naval station, the expenditure for which is for Imperial purposes; and General Sir J. F. Burgoyne, Inspector-General of fortifications, in his evidence, gives it as his opinion that Kingston and Quebec, as well as Halifax, should be maintained in Imperial interest, and in the recent debate (March 23, 1864) in the House of Commons on the appropriation for the defence of Quebec, Lord Palmerston urged the vote on the ground that 'this was not a Canadian question, it was not a local question, it was an Imperial question,' and the House sanctioned this view by a majority of 275 to 40. The five Australian colonies are down for £226,397; but of course they were not exposed to danger from foreign enemies, and New Zealand alone from domestic. But the heaviest expenditure even under the first-class, was for Ceylon, Mauritius, the South African and West India colonies, which make up £1,075,273 of the £1,715,246, leaving but £639,973 for the North American and Australian dependencies, those great and flourishing communities chiefly of our own kith and kin. And for their own defence the colonies had appropriated £369,224, all, excepting £7,901, from the first-class, still further reducing this insignificant sum of little more than half a million set against provinces which furnish a trade of seventy millions; and even from this must be taken heavy sums for naval stations and other 'expenses not colonial,' which would be greater in purely Imperial interests if there were no such colonies, affording shelter to British shipping and protection to British commerce in the Atlantic, Pacific, South and Indian seas. Upon this part of the Report, too, the Committee state, that 'large sums appear to have been received from the colonial governments by Imperial officers for strictly military purposes as to which no accounts have been rendered to the War Office or the Treasury.'

If all the most momentous interests of a vast empire are to be summed up in the annual balance-sheet, there will be other items to set against the Imperial account. The British navy is not kept in those distant waters, as one class of writers flippantly asserts, to defend the colonies or colonial interests, so much as to protect British commerce. Where there are British ports and loyal populations, commerce requires little else for its protection.

'The trade of Australia is forty millions, almost all of which, when at sea and in the harbours, is British property, and entirely insured at home. The interest which the colonies have in it is very small indeed' (*Mr. Merivale's ev.* 2346–2350.)

Canada had a trade in 1863 of nearly ninety millions of dollars, and the British provinces in the valley of the St. Lawrence, of some thirty millions sterling. The shipping of Canada, Nova Scotia, and New Brunswick, amounted to twelve millions of tons. 'These figures represented a trade,' says Mr. Galt, Finance Minister of Canada, 'which is probably the third in the world, exceeded only by the trade of Great Britain and the United States, and, perhaps, the trade of France, which last, however, did not much, if at all, exceed the figures just given.'

Where, in the history of commerce, have such mighty results grown from such insignificant expenditure as in the colonial trade of Great Britain? Half a million is drawn from the British exchequer for Canada and Australia, whose trade counts up to seventy millions. If these were mere trading posts, kept up by commercial houses, the result would be considered a magnificent commercial undertaking.

British capital, British shipping, and British manufactures enter largely into this vast trade. Those friendly populations and protecting ports make this commerce safe almost without the aid of the British navy. 'The naval expenditure,' says Earl Grey (*Col. Policy*, 1*st Letter*, p. 43), 'which is frequently charged against the colonies, cannot, in my opinion, be so with any justice, since if we had no colonies, I believe that the demands upon our naval force would be rather increased than diminished, from the necessity of protecting our commerce.'

If this be true in peace, what would be the effect in war, were those colonies independent, or, may be, provinces of a hostile Power? If the West India Islands had been United States' territory in the present American war, how much easier her task to blockade Southern ports and defend her commerce. A recent estimate gives the destruction of property on the ocean by Southern privateers at £100,000,000, without including the loss to the nation by her commerce being driven from the seas. Supposing again British America to be independent, not to say a State of the American Union, in a war between England and those States, would British commerce and British interests be safer in those waters than now? Would Imperial expenditure be less than now, when all the power of a vigorous population of four millions of true and ardent allies, men of the same bone and muscle and spirit as ourselves, would be put forth by land and sea in attacks on a frontier of thousands of miles; not thousands of miles for Britain to defend—for that Canadians have heretofore done when much weaker comparatively than now—but thousands of miles from which to attack an exposed frontier, thousands of miles for the enemy to defend, dividing his forces and exhausting his strength. Even granting the assumption that British America could be conquered, Britain then, according to the dicta of these timid people, would be stronger than before, and the enemy, after all his waste of men and material, would, at his own expense and to his own detriment, have done the empire the highest service. Britain would henceforth be strong and America weak.

'Canada is a source of weakness to us,' say these profound reasoners. 'With half the American continent against us, and Canada for us, we are in danger. Let but Canada join the Republic, we shall then have the whole continent, with its implacable population, against us, and shall again be safe.'

British America is, of all the countries on that continent, the least likely to be conquered. In position she is a Russia. A campaign can be carried on only in summer. She can be attacked only from the south, and, if defeated, has more than Scythian fastnesses in her Ottawas, her Saguenay, and her lake regions. Her population is certainly as hardy, as self-relying, as proud-spirited as any on that continent, trained to the use of arms, and accustomed to all those manly exercises, the best school for the soldier in a country of countless lakes, of vast forests, and of great and numerous rivers. She is yet, it is true, sparsely settled, but the census gives to her population and wealth a more rapid increase during the last twenty-five years than even to the most favoured regions of the renowned Republic. In the fertility of her soil, the salubrity of her climate, in her minerals, her forests, and fisheries on her coasts and gulfs and inland waters, the materials of wealth abound. Situated in that portion of the temperate zone most propitious to the grains and grasses, the favoured regions of the ox, the sheep, and the horse, wealth and material prosperity are her sure inheritance. In none of the institutions of the neighbouring Republic, as compared with her own, does she know anything to envy. She had been insensible to the taunts of her Republican neighbours and their British sympathizers when less prosperous, knowing, too, as she did, that British capital and British labour sent by British subjects to the Republic were the grounds of that contrast; she has repelled, by force, the many attempts to subject her to the Republic, and had many things to complain of in her colonial position, reminding her almost, especially in the past, that to be a colonist was to have passed under the *Caudine forks*. Under such circumstances, British America has been true to herself, and true to the Crown. Her past gives no ground of fear that she can ever be turned from her allegiance by aught but the want of wisdom in the rulers of the empire.

The civil expenditure on colonial account is now reduced to the salaries of some of the West India governors, and to the maintenance of one or two trifling settlements which do not pay expenses. These are purely questions of colonial policy, unconnected with the general principles of the colonial empire.

The previous estimate for colonial expenditure, military, naval, convict, anti-slavery, &c. was for the year ending March 31, 1860. Reference is here made to another, that of 1857 (*printed in Parliamentary Report*, 1859), for the purpose mainly of introducing the admirable remarks of Mr. Merivale, for twelve years Under-Secretary of State for the Colonies.

The total military expenditure on account of colonies, is estimated by Messrs. Hamilton, Godley, and Elliot in 1857 at £3,600,000, but this large return includes several charges, such as transport and freight, proportion of departmental expenses, &c. not heretofore brought into account. From this sum should be deducted £1,100,000, for the Mediterranean and other garrisons not properly colonial. Out of the residue, £2,500,000, £800,000 were absorbed by the Cape of Good Hope alone.

Military expenditure is incurred in colonies

(whether defrayed by the mother country or by the colonies) for three distinct purposes :—

1. For prevention against foreign war with civilized Powers;
2. For maintenance of internal tranquillity;
3. For precaution against the hostility of natives.

For the second and third of these objects no expenses of the Imperial Exchequer are incurred for any of the great colonies proper, unless it may be temporarily at the Cape and in New Zealand. But if the case of New Zealand, of which so much has been said, and so bitterly said, proves anything, it is either that the natives are superior to those of other countries settled by British colonists, or else that the British colonists of the present day in New Zealand are inferior to those of former days. The natives, as in other colonies, have been under the special supervision of the Imperial authorities, and these, and not the colonists, are responsible for the results. Had the entire matter been left with those on the spot, it would never have reached the present state. The first of these objects—precaution against foreign war—it has been usual in British policy to consider as of Imperial interest, although one school of British politicians would have the colonies defend themselves. Surely while the mother country conducts the foreign relations of her dependencies, she is responsible for the consequences of that diplomacy. She may draw them into disastrous wars, or subject them to an ignominious peace, on questions in which they have no concern, as in the war of 1812, or where their territories are sacrificed as the price of peace, as in the Ashburton treaty of 1846. While those international relations touch only upon questions of peace, the honour in negotiations of interests so vast belongs all to the parent State. But if she will enjoy the luxury of all the diplomacy for the empire in peace, she cannot rid herself of the responsibility in war. The Duke of Newcastle expressed himself strongly upon this point. 'As a general rule, it is undoubtedly the duty of this country to protect our colonial possessions from foreign aggression at all hazards and at all expense.' (*Hansard*, Feb. 1864.)

Upon the annual expenditure for colonial purposes Mr. Merivale well remarks:—

'*But it is essential to disabuse the public mind of the common and superficial notion that what appears in the public returns as colonial military expenditure is really such, except in a very small proportion. This great community is no longer limited in these days of vast but only beginning expansion, by local bounds. Every sea has its British population carrying the trade of Britain. Every foreign country, almost every frequented port, has its colony of British* residents with their commercial property. And in every region of the world we have our political interests, real or imaginary. *Now it is to protect this trade, these fellow-subjects* and their interests, not to protect the people of Malta, Gibraltar, Mauritius, Hong Kong, that these ports and others are occupied by expensive British garrisons. Whether such expenditure be wise or foolish, is not the purpose of our present inquiry; *it is sufficient that it is not colonial.* Adding to such places as those named a few others where the expenditure is really incurred for convict, not colonial purposes, and other factories for mixed trading and anti-slavery purposes, we arrive at a deduction of more than £1,500,000 from the sum of £3,500,000, at which the Report estimates " Imperial expenditure for military purposes."

'Of the remaining £2,000,000, one-fourth [£500,000, and in 1860, £413,000] is appropriated to the North American colonies. In these great colonies, no danger from natives is possible. The whole amount must therefore be regarded as insurance against foreign invasion. And as such, the colonies urge that it ought to fall upon the mother country to contribute largely towards their security. "We," they say, "have no interest in provoking foreign wars. If ever we are engaged in them it will be in consequence of Imperial quarrels, not of our own. And besides this, your expensive fortresses of Quebec and Halifax are, in reality, rather posts for the protection of your own interests, like Malta or Gibraltar, than for the colonial purposes of Canada or Nova Scotia."

'The expenditure incurred for the defence of the colonies by the Imperial Government in 1858, and one of remarkable quiet throughout our colonial empire, was for defence of posts for military, convict, commercial, and other special purposes, £1,600,000
Of colonial against foreign Powers simply   400,000
Against foreign Powers and internal
   disturbances, but chiefly the latter   .   600,000
Against warlike natives 1,000,000

                       Total £3,600,000

'Not content,' says Mr. Adderley (p. 31), 'with relieving the strength of such a colony (Canada) of the task of defending its wealth, we further contribute to its wealth, by paying Canadian bishops, rectors, and archdeacons, although the Crown has given up the sales of clergy-lands, which were expressly reserved for that purpose.' 'We assist Canada,' says the 'Times,' January 23, 1863, 'to pay its archdeacons and its clergy.' This is a peculiarly English view founded on imperfect information. Canada has no established Church, and therefore, as a State, has no bishops, archbishops, and clergy. Those payments referred to were never made from the clergy-lands, but were originally engagements by the Crown in pursuance of the Imperial policy to establish the Church of England by law in Canada. This was contemplated

'The contrast between the present and former colonies,' is the burden of the song of one class of writers on colonial questions. Mr. Adderley gives us a chapter on it, and makes it the basis of his pamphlet. The Reports of Parliamentary Committees are full of it. The press and the Parliament have re-echoed it, but all in the most vague generalities. The natives in one of the islands of the South Seas are dissatisfied with their bargain with the Home Government, for it is the Crown which has special charge of their affairs. Mr. Adderley quotes the opinions of the Prime Minister at Auckland on the policy which has led to the war: 'It is a complication of folly and wickedness—a simple confusion—an abomination.' Troops are sent from England. Then comes the sweeping charge in Parliament, in pamphlets, and in the press—' Colonists of to-day are not made of the same stuff as of old.' So of the Cape. There are fifty

in the Act of 1791, and it had taken Canada from that date until 1854 to rid herself of it. This it was which caused the rebellion in Upper Canada in 1837. Of the clergy-lands referred to by Mr. Adderley as Crown property, it is sufficient to state, that the Canadian House of Assembly on numerous occasions, extending over a period of thirty or forty years, voted to appropriate them to general education, or to throw them into the public funds, on the ground that, made valuable by the labour of the public, they should be given to the public, and not to a party.

dependencies, differing from each other as widely as fifty independent nations. Yet an isolated occurrence in one is made the basis of condemning the whole. The old American colonies, it is said, defended themselves against the natives, made war upon the French in the West Indies, Port Royal in 1710, and Cape Breton in 1745. Mr. Godley, 'whose mind,' Mr. Adderley informs us, ' has furnished all the wisdom I may have collected on this subject,' states in his evidence,—

'They (old American colonies) had, as an immediate neighbour, a far more formidable Power, for aggressive purposes, than the United States, viz. the French, and on the other side a more formidable naval and military Power, the Spaniards; so that the danger to our New England colonies *from foreign aggression was infinitely greater than the danger of Canada from aggression by the United States.*' (2195.)

It would be difficult to conceive a more preposterous statement than the one here made. There was little danger to those old colonies from the fleets of either of these powers while England could meet them on the sea. The French settlements were chiefly on the Lower St. Lawrence; the English on the seaboard, separated by hundreds of miles of rough country without roads, covered by vast forests, tenanted by numerous tribes of Indians, each hostile to his neighbour. The force which the French could send to such a distance was quite insignificant. The troops of New England, which conquered Halifax, Nova Scotia, and Cape Breton, quoted so often as examples of the prowess of the old colonies, were ten to one in force to the regulars opposed to them. Mr. Adderley himself has shown the absurdity of Mr. Godley's statement in his lament that 'we have felt it (United States) act, on important points of international policy, upon ourselves of late, *influencing, attracting, repelling, controlling from afar.*' So the 'Times' (January 24, 1863) asserts, 'that the United States insults with impunity by turns every Power of the European continent.' It is true that the 'Times' had complained the day before that 'Canada does not defend herself against the United States,' but this Mr. Adderley himself does while standing in awe of that overshadowing Power. Yet Canada has always held her ground against every attack from even the Great Republic, grown to twenty times the strength it was when, in detached communities with no roads but the Indian path, it defended itself from the aborigines, themselves divided into innumerable tribes, neutralizing each other's power by their deadly enmities. Now those model all-conquering old colonies have become a mighty Power; their railways and canals touch the Canadas at a hundred points; they are filled with a turbulent population, the socialists, the republicans, the propagandists of the old world, ready for a tilt anywhere against anybody connected with a monarchy. It is no small credit that Canada has maintained a defiant attitude when threatened, and repelled the many attacks of such a Power—a Power which 'overawes,' which 'insults' with impunity every nation of Europe.' 'Mr. Godley refers,' says Mr. Merivale, 'to the early history of the New England colonies, that before 1754, when regular forces were first maintained in them, had not only defended themselves, but conquered Nova Scotia and Cape Breton for England. All this is true, but, unfortunately, it is one of those truths which are most effective when clothed in general language, and lose most of their force when we change the ground from generals to particulars. The old English colonies had no foreign enemies, except France. All that was needed was that England should be practically as near to them as France. At the present day, the menace, against which the British troops are thought to guard, proceeds, not from France, but from the United States, the country of a powerful and warlike people, contemporaneous with our provinces for thousands of miles.'

The Select Committee of 1861 sought information upon this point from all or nearly all who came before them, but except a mere theorist or two, all repudiated the idea of there being any analogy between the two cases.

'Did not the old colonies,' asked Mr. Mills' Committee of Earl Grey, 'undertake the primary responsibility of their own defence, England contributing? now England undertakes the primary responsibility, and calls upon the colonies to contribute.' 'I do not know,' was Earl Grey's reply, 'whether that is a correct way of describing it. At that time the whole state of the world was so different to what it is now, that you can hardly draw any comparison between the two. The colonies were not attacked upon their own grounds by the great armies of civilized Powers; their principal danger was from Indian tribes, or from irregular forces of the French. The French troops were very small indeed.'

'The colonial troops,' says General Burgoyne, 'which conquered Nova Scotia, Halifax, and Cape Breton, were ten to one in force to the regulars opposed to them.' (*Ev.* 1356.)

If Canada had always been, compared with the Republic on her border, ten to one, instead of one to twenty, as in 1812, and one to twelve or fourteen in 1860; if she had, like the old colonies, and subsequently the United States, been at first the leading and afterwards almost the only Power on that continent, these comparisons of Mr. Godley and Mr. Adderley would have weight; but as the facts really are they completely misstate—directly reverse—the question. As early as 1660 the population of the British colonies in America is estimated at 80,000, as large a number as the French in Canada a century later, which are placed in 1763 at 65,000 in the province of Quebec, and about 30,000 in the remaining districts, Trois Rivières, Montreal, and the Lakes. While in 1763 the English colonists must have numbered more than 1,500,000 (twelve years after we find them nearly 3,000,000); Massachusetts alone having 240,000, Pennsylvania 280,000, and Massachusetts and Connecticut—the two states nearest Canada—400,000, as against 60,000 or 70,000 French in the latter province. That neither the French nor Spanish in America ever interfered seriously with the English settlements, ought to have prevented any impartial and ingenuous writer from instituting such comparisons, and must now, that they are made, be considered a sufficient answer to them. The United States have really been the most aggressive Power of the age, not excepting even Russia. The first charters of the London and Plymouth companies, organizing Virginia and Massachusetts, the two great centres from which the Republic has grown to its enormous dimensions, give only 100 miles inland. First the natives were deprived of their lands. Louisiana was purchased in 1803 for $15,000,000 from France, and Florida ceded in 1821 by Spain; Texas, California, and vast territories lying between them, were wrested from Mexico. Upon Cuba and Central America attempts have been twice made by fillibusters from the United States, whom their Government did little to check. On the north, in the first treaty on the boundary line, after they had gained their independence, immense British territory from the Lakes to the Pacific was ceded; also in the second—the 'Ashburton'—large portions of Canada, New Brunswick, and an important island in the St. Lawrence, controlling the river, the Canadian canals and railways; 200 miles of the northern shore of Lake Superior and the island Royal—the Malta of the Lake; and vast regions thence to the Pacific; portions of Oregon and other territory in the Pacific; were surrendered to avoid a war. Maine, ceded in the same treaty, and running like a wedge between Canada and the maritime provinces, lies an impassible barrier between the ocean and those great countries in the valley of the St. Lawrence and the regions west.

In 1775 and in 1812, Canada was invaded by

American troops, and in 1837 by 'sympathizers.' The defence of Canada is the defence of British America. Britain thought it good policy to send her army and her fleet for the defence of Turkey against Russia, at an expense of £100,000,000, but when a few troops are garrisoned in Canada, no language seems too strong in condemnation of a colony allowing itself to receive them to aid, if necessary, in her defence. Every Power of Europe is concerned in checking the encroachments of Russia, Britain alone of European States is affected by the aggressions of the mammoth Power of the West. Canada, as an integral part of the empire, would, with the confederacy on the south, create a balance of power on that continent. Already the mercantile marine of the British North American Provinces on the St. Lawrence and Atlantic, is the fourth, if not the third, in tonnage amongst the nations of the earth; and the mercantile marine is the basis of the navy. Her vast fisheries on the Atlantic, in the Gulf and Great Lakes, are the most admirable school for the navy. Her sailors and fishermen number 70,000. Her sons now enter the British army and navy. A regiment was offered by Canada at the time of the Crimean war and given since (the 100th); another is being raised for the Crown. Her cordial, earnest British feeling has been shown in every war, and in every calamity that has befallen the mother country. Britain makes all her calculations upon the basis of her supremacy at sea. The British colonists in every part of the globe are equally with the sons of these islands a mercantile people, and go down to the sea in great ships. Britain must be mistress of the seas; that's a necessity for her. With the mighty navies now growing up on both sides of the Atlantic, no light weight in the scales will be what these vigorous offshoots can add, in the gift of their sons, their fleets, and their friendly ports.

Those English writers who admit the importance of colonies to the mother country usually assume, for they give us no proof of their assertions, that the advantages of the connection are mostly in favour of the colonies. The chief of these advantages to them is their defence. We do not under-estimate the might of England and the potency of her protecting shield over the distant members of the empire. Doubtless an enemy would not, without a weighty cause, wake that power into action. But we do not place all their safety from attacks to the credit of their Imperial connection. States smaller even than those infant countries live by the side of the great military Powers of Europe without molestation, and without being often involved in foreign quarrels. If the North American, the Australian, and South

African colonies were sovereign States, there is only one nation of Europe, or at most only two, that could endanger their independence. And the motives for such molestation are not easily to be perceived. Canada is the only one of the dependencies of the Crown yet drawn into foreign wars, and these have been solely through the follies of British statesmen, and must be credited to their connection with England. At this day there is a much more friendly feeling between Canada and her neighbour than between England and that Republic, and, as the only wars of that colony have been brought upon her by being involved in the foreign policy of the mother country, her danger could scarcely be considered greater after severing the connection. It is a mistake, too, to assume that the colonies, if cast off by England, would be friendless. Their immense trade would secure them allies.

What really are the great advantages to those thriving communities of a continued colonial position? The English, the Germans, the Scandinavians, the migrating races of the old world, go chiefly to the United States. British capital follows them there more than elsewhere for investment. The mother country subsidizes two lines of steamers to New York and Boston, instead of to Halifax and Quebec, and has refused even one penny to a Canadian line.

Trade with the Republic is thus fostered at the expense of that with British colonies, while the trade of these contributes vastly more than that of the Republic to the wealth of the nation in proportion to their populations. The statesmen, too, of those countries, while dependencies of the Crown, are virtually confined to the narrow circle of mere municipalities. We say virtually. The Crown might be an impartial distributor, an equal fountain of honour, to its subjects in every part of the empire; but favour is merit, and this kind of merit is most appreciated near the throne.

The existence of numerous, ardent, and faithful allies in every part of the globe contributes greatly to the protection of the commerce of Britain, carried on on every sea and in every port and navigable river, lessens instead of increases those expenses of the navy incurred for the defence of trade, and adds to the moral influence and strength of the empire. They provide new and congenial homes for the surplus population of the mother country, and new fields for the employment of British capital, under the more stable government and greater protection of British institutions, where capital and labour are most productive. They are still saved to the empire, and they contribute more than any other populations to swell the commerce of the nation; and, although beyond the seas, add vastly to the value of every man's estate, and to every artisan's and labourer's profits in the kingdom.

If we were to measure the advantages to the parent State from the colonies, because they are colonies, by the profits of trade alone, the result would be an enormous sum, both absolutely and compared with the expenditure on colonial account. Earl Chatham declared in 1766 that 'the profits to Great Britain from the trade of the colonies is two millions a year. This is the fund that carried you triumphantly through the last war. The estates that were at two thousand pounds a year threescore years ago are at three thousand pounds at present. You owe this to America. This is the price America pays you for her protection. I dare not say how much higher the profits may be augmented.'

A century has passed since the utterance of these words; a century of profits enjoyed from that trade, and of dangers escaped by the relief through emigration to an over-burdened population. Six millions and a half of people have gone from the United Kingdom since 1800, and the pressure of population on subsistence has been relieved to that extent in the first instance, and the nation saved from the accumulated pressure of the numbers to which the six and a half millions would have grown.

Population increases more rapidly than the means of subsistence: in the United Kingdom it doubles itself in twenty-five years. The dangers that have been escaped and the good done by this free and copious emigration are beyond computation—a good alike to those left behind and to those who have gone where labour is more productive and capital reaps a better profit, and where, therefore, as consumers they take more largely of British goods, and as producers contribute more to British trade than they would if they had stayed in these islands or gone to foreign countries. They, too, remain loyal British subjects. Their increase in wealth and population will be so much added to the wealth, population, and strength of the empire.

'This great field' (the United States), says Mr. Merivale, 'for emigration seems to be closed. Even a restored union, if such a thing be possible, must go through a struggle of years, from its present calamities, before it can be attractive to the emigrant as heretofore. Few I think have at all realized the nature and magnitude of the evil which is impending over us from the closing, even for a time, of that outlet for our superabundant population. It was a safety-valve always open. Periods of comparative depression here, such as rendered emigration more desirable, were seldom coincident with periods of comparative depression in the States. Emigration has been the regular provision for one child in six born in this part of the United Kingdom; but in Ireland more nearly for one in three. Those must be far more sanguine than I am who can look without great apprehension at the threatened abolition of that provision, or at least much more than half of it—being the proportion which the States have hitherto offered.

'And it surely follows that continued colonization and the continuance also of our political relation with such colonies as we possess, are more than ever important to the well-being of the community. Canada, as long as it remains connected with us, affords a certain and regular place of resort for no inconsiderable portion of our surplus. How long Canada might do so if we were to follow the advice of a modern political school, by leaving her to independence—that is, to forming connection with the States—no wise man, with the civil war raging before his eyes, will venture to anticipate. Emigration to Australia and New Zealand is carried on at a greater disadvantage, still it has carried off on the average one-eighth of our surplus since 1825, and will carry off a great deal more. Let us withdraw from Australia the British flag, and it is highly improbable, in all ordinary political calculations, that emigration would continue to anything like the same amount when the sense of security now felt under British institutions had ceased to exist. The greater the loss, in short, which the sufferings of the American Republic have inflicted on us and on the world, the greater the importance of keeping our hold on those substitutes which have been left us, and of which the mutual value is as yet undeveloped.' (*Merivale on the Utility of Colonies, read at Cambridge Br. As. Sec.* (F), 1862.)

'The benefit of colonies to the mother country consists solely in the surplus advantages which it derives from the trade of the colonies over the loss. *That benefit has been enormous, calculated in figures alone.* The imports from our colonies amount to £26,000,000 (£5 5s. per person). From the United States, equally the result of British colonization, £34,000,000 (£1 2s. 6d. per person. But of bread-stuffs imported from the United States, a large per centage—nearly one-half—is Canadian.) From all the rest of the world, including our Indian possessions, £114,000,000.' (*Average of* 1856-8. *Merivale's Lectures*, p. 672.)

'It is plain that the clear pecuniary loss of Great Britain from the retention of her North American empire is confined wholly to the sums which may have been spent by the British Treasury in its government and defence. These I have already had occasion to show are much overrated in public estimation; and are partially, though of course not wholly, compensated by the increase of local wealth and trade produced by government expenditure.' (*Average of 1856–8. Merivale's Lectures, p. 673.*)

Mr. Laing, late Finance Minister of India, in a lecture on the 'Trade and Finance of the British Empire' for 1863, delivered at Wick, in September 1864, has given some very important facts on this subject.

'Who,' he asks, 'are our chief customers? In the first place, I observe that our own possessions are by far our best customers. Together they furnish very nearly one-third of our import trade, and one-half our export trade! British India stands for the first in the list, giving us nearly £50,000,000 of imports, and taking in return £20,000,000 of exports. For the current year (1864) these figures will be considerably exceeded, and the rate of progression is most marked, the imports ten years ago having been only £10,672,000, and the exports £9,620,000. Australia shows a wonderful result, considering its recent settlement and limited population. It sends us, exclusive of gold, about £7,000,000 of imports, and takes £13,000,000 of exports. The North American colonies, with a similar British population, give us £8,000,000 of imports, and takes nearly £5,000,000 of exports. The little island of Mauritius, with the advantage of British government and capital, sends us nearly £2,000,000 a year, and takes £500,000. These instances apparently show the advantages of colonies to commerce, and refute the shallow theory which asks us to abandon our distant possessions as useless appendages. It is true that we no longer impose a monopoly, and leave them free as air to sell in the dearest and buy in the cheapest market; but it is no less true that the tendency of trade is always towards the mother country, and that a given population, whether it be of British origin, as in Australia or Canada, or of foreign race, as in India or Ceylon, will always furnish a larger trade per head with Great Britain, if they form part of the British empire, than if, as in the United States or in China, they are subjects of a foreign government.'

The trade* for 1863, imports and exports, with France was £42,000,000; with Russia, £18,000,000; with Turkey, £10,000,000; Prussia and North Germany, £32,000,000; Holland, £18,000,000; Belgium, £9,000,000; Spain, £6,500,000; Cuba, £6,000,000; Brazil, £8,000,000; United States

---

* The trade, imports and exports, for 1863, amounted, with France, to about £1 1s. per head of her population; with Germany, to 15s.; with Russia, 5s.; Turkey and Spain, 6s.; Belgium, £1 8s.; Brazil, £1; United States, £1 4s. (£2 in 1860); Australia (exclusive of gold), £14; North American Colonies, £4. The trade with Holland was chiefly *in transitu*.

(before the war, £60,000,000), £40,000,000; Australia, exclusive of gold, £20,000,000; North American Colonies, £13,000,000. In estimating the imports from the United States and the British North American provinces into Britain, it must be borne in mind that the chief markets for Canadian bread-stuffs are New England and New York. Out of the 60,000,000 bushels of grain of all kinds which have left the Canadian Lakes annually for several years, 50,000,000, and until very recently at all events 55,000,000, have gone to the States. Whether this is exported or consumed there and releases American grain, the result is the same; it is quoted as American, lessening by so much Canadian exports. For many years Canada has exported as much wheat of her own growth as the whole of the United States. Neither New England nor the South grow wheat, or only to a very limited extent; the central States, the only ones with a surplus, can scarcely supply the deficiency in those States—more than a score—which do not produce their own; while Upper Canada alone has sent to the States from 10,000,000 to 20,000,000 bushels of wheat a year.

Emigrants who go to the colonies take of British manufactures £7 6s. 10½d. per head; those who go to the United States take but 17s. per head.—(*Reports of Col. Em. So.*)

From 1815 to 1860, 3,100,000 emigrants went from Great Britain to the American Republic alone, and 2,040,000 to all the fifty colonies. The amount of imports into three North American and seven Australian colonies in 1861 was about £18,000,000. The English manufacturer, besides all his costs in manufacturing these goods, must add to them the proportion which they should bear of his part of the national debt and national expenditure. These the consumer in the distant dependency pays; and as that consumer takes more largely of British manufactures abroad than he did at home, he pays on these goods more to the national exchequer than before he left these shores. The 3,100,000 British subjects who have gone to the United States, supposing them to have migrated at once, would take in one year £2,635,000 worth of British goods; while the 2,040,000 to the colonies would take £14,670,000 worth; and if the 3,100,000 had gone to the colonies, instead of to the United States, they would take of British manufactures £22,300,000 worth, instead of £2,600,000 as now. Yet it is British capitalists chiefly who are responsible for so many British subjects going to the United States instead of to the colonies. Had they gone to the colonies, they and their descendants would have continued to take of British goods the larger proportion. What an enormous sum would be represented by the difference between what these now contribute to British commerce and British manufactures, and what they and their descendants would contribute, if their steps had been directed to the British colonies!

We are told, too, that the cost of defending this vast commerce is much less on those friendly shores than a similar trade would be in foreign countries. British commerce in Chinese or Brazilian waters is not so safe as in Australian and Canadian. Where the trade is less, the insurance is heavier and the cost to the navy greater.

Franklin, in his evidence before the House of Commons in 1766, gave it as his opinion that the intercourse between the mother country and the colonies created in the minds of the colonists a fondness for English fashions, which conduced greatly to the increase of trade. French fashions and French fabrics have, since the Revolution, been adopted in America, to a much greater extent than amongst any English-speaking population.

The whole export trade of Britain, including that of her colonies, in 1704, was but £6,509,000; that of Canada alone, in 1861, was £8,700,000, and her imports £9,500,000. Victoria (1861) had £12,298,882 exports, and £13,215,166 imports; and New South Wales £5,072,020 exports, and £7,519,285 imports.

Countries that but a few years ago were known only as the hunting ground of the savage, amusing us only with the accounts of new and strange races of men, are now the happy homes of well-ordered and prosperous communities, having a commerce greater than the whole of Britain a century and a half ago. The population of Great Britain was stated by Lord North in 1775 to have been 8,000,000; that of the British provinces in the valley of the St. Lawrence in 1865 is 4,000,000; a century before they were estimated at not more than 120,000.

In the important debate on the defences of Canada in the House of Commons on the 23rd of March, the Under-Secretary of War, the Marquis of Hartington, laid before the House the views of the Government on this question, furnished upon the report of Lieutenant Colonel Jervois, Deputy Inspector-General of Fortifications. Colonel Jervois had recommended £200,000 for the defence of Quebec, and £443,000 for Montreal. The former of these sums the British Government proposes to pay, leaving the other, that for the defences of Montreal, to the Canadian Government, as also £500,000 towards fortifications for Kingston, Toronto, and Hamilton. The Under-Secretary of War states on behalf of the Government, that the defence of the works at Quebec and Montreal would require a force of 12,000 men; but in case of an attack on those points, it would be desirable to have at least 35,000 men, and further, a movable force of 20,000 to 25,000 to harass the enemy. The total force that would be required for the defence of the Lower St. Lawrence to Montreal would be 60,000 men. We could easily, the Under-Secretary of War states, send out from this country 20,000 troops; there are already 20,000 volunteers enrolled and organized in Canada, and 80,000 designated and by the law of the country required to turn out; or, as the Secretary for the colonies stated, 89,000 had already been balloted for. These, with their officers, would make a force of 100,000. Thus we could bring into the field at once 120,000 men; Mr. Disraeli says 200,000. The Canadians have half a million of men capable of bearing arms, mostly accustomed to the use of the rifle, and to those hardy pursuits eminently qualifying them for military duty.

Colonel Jervois gives it as his opinion that, 'owing to the length and nature of the frontier of Canada, it was impossible to protect it throughout its whole extent; an enemy must nevertheless acquire possession of certain vital points before he could obtain any military advantage; that there are only a few such points; and that, if proper arrangements were made for the defence of those places by the construction of fortifications, the provision of gunboats, and the improvement of communications, the militia and volunteer forces of the country, if properly organized, and aided by British troops, would be enabled to hold them during the period, only about six months in the year, when military operations on a large scale could be carried on against them, and thus those forces could resist an attack with the best possible chance of success.' These views the Government have adopted after consultation with the most experienced and able men in the service. Their proposal to expend one-fifth of a million in four years for purposes so important, while we have laid out ten millions in five years on our own coast, Parliament might well sanction without a murmur. At the close of the debate Lord Palmerston urged upon the House 'that as the tone and line of argument were so much in favour of the motion, it would be very undesirable that there should appear to be a difference of opinion. It is a question,' he said, 'which affects the position and character, the honour, the interests, and the duties of this great country. It has been said[*] that you can't defend Canada. Now I utterly deny that proposition.' Equally explicit was the Secretary of the Colonies in stating the opinions of the Government. 'My right hon.

---

[*] By Mr. Lowe.

friend (Mr. Lowe) has said that in this debate no one has ventured to assert the contrary of the proposition which he has laid down, and to maintain that Canada can be defended. I should rather have said, after listening attentively to every word in this debate, that until my right hon. friend himself rose almost the whole discussion had been upon one side, and there was nothing for those who support the vote to reply to except the argument of my right hon. friend.'* So also Mr. Disraeli on behalf of the Opposition. 'Those provinces, and the lands contiguous to them, have the means of sustaining not only millions but tens of millions of population. Canada has, I believe, its own future before it. It has all the elements which make a nation.' 'Our North American provinces,' says the Under-Secretary of War, 'are a great nation, and are on the high road to be a still greater nation.'

Those who in the House and in the press have so earnestly urged that Canada cannot be defended in Canada, that our only means of defending her is by our fleet, in attacking the United States at their most vulnerable parts, assume that we shall certainly have command of the sea, and that American privateers could inflict little injury on our commerce in com-

* Speech of the Right Hon. Mr. Cardwell, March 23, 1865.

parison with the damage we could do them. Surely, too, if we cannot defend Canadian soil with the assistance of 100,000 or 200,000 militia, we can have little hope of success in any attack upon the American seaboard where we shall have no such assistance. The conquest of Canada, admitting that to be possible, would require the entire military force of the United States. It would then be good policy to make that task as difficult of execution as possible, for upon it the enemy must employ a vast army, which would disperse his forces and exhaust his strength. Supposing Britain should have such supremacy of the seas as to be able to inflict without receiving blows, the Americans would probably allow the few towns that could be reached to be destroyed, consoling themselves with the reflection that we were destroying as much English as American property, while their privateers would retaliate upon our commerce. If the States attack Canada, they must be prepared to defend their own frontiers of some 2,000 miles; they must have sufficient force for defence as well as for attack; and the war of 1812–15 shows that Canada, then comparatively much weaker than now, could inflict more damage than she received.

Canada has now been British for more than a century, but has never involved the parent State in hostilities. War and the dangers of war have come not from the land but from the sea, and those over-provident statesmen who would surrender English provinces lest offence might be given to other nations by holding them, would be more consistent were they to advise the surrender of the sea, for thence have sprung the *casus belli*. The war of 1812–15 grew out of the conflict of English and American interests at sea and not in Canada; the Trent affair of 1861, for which England would have gone to war, was one of the sea and not of the land; and the now pending claims for the destruction of American commerce by privateers built in English dockyards—claims which, if pressed, as threatened, must end in war, originated in acts committed on the seas and not on land. In Indian and Chinese, in Japanese and Australian waters, in every sea and on every coast, English and American commerce and opposing interests are much more likely to endanger the peaceful relations of the two countries than any questions of provinces. Those amiable people, in their desire to conciliate the goodwill of powerful nations, would therefore get the credit of reason in their pusillanimity by giving up the sea, instead of attempting to propitiate by the sacrifice of provinces, which could not avert the apprehended danger.

CHAPTER IX.

OPINIONS, IMPERIAL AND COLONIAL.

I. Is it interest that binds Colonies to the Parent State?—Position of Canada and England reversed—II. Does England draw the Colonies, or the Colonies England, into war?—English and French Policy as a Peace Policy—United States towards England and France—Mr. Adderley—Earl Grey—The Cape—New Zealand—III. Institutions Ecclesiastical and Civil of Old Countries and New—IV. Canada during the Civil War in America—Mr. Adderley—Harsh and Hasty Opinions—Foreign Policy—Influence on Canada of a Confederation on its Border free from Slavery—England's Relations to Slave-holding Countries—Duke of Newcastle—V. Colonial Systems—Past and Present—Mr. Adderley's Reviewer—English Writers on 'High Spirit' and International Duties—Gladstone—VI. Cost of Colonies—Trade in Comparison with Cost—Troops—Newcastle—Grey—New Zealand—Cape—Archdeacons and Clergy Reserves of Canada—VII. Old Colonies—Policy of English Statesmen—VIII. Imperial Interests, how Represented in Colonies; and Colonial in Mother Country—IX. Policy Recommended by Committee of 1861—Godley—Merivale—Policy Suggested by Circumstances—No Rigid Rule—Newcastle—Grey—X. Mr. Adderley's Contrast between Old and New Colonies—Virginia—Canada—Attributes Acts of Old Colonies to wrong Motives—Old Colonies feared Parliament and Crown; and England the too rapid Growth of Colonies. Pp. 129–165.

1. Is it interest that binds the colonies to the parent State? Earl Grey gives it as his opinion that

these faithful allies add strength to the empire, that the expense of the navy would be greater if there were no colonies, from the greater necessity of defending British commerce. All admit, as Franklin did, a century ago, that English manufactures are taken to a larger extent by countries under British rule, and trade is greater with them. In war the mother country has their moral support, and, if need be, their material aid. But colonists may be involved in the most devastating wars solely because of their relation to Britain. Australia was recently threatened with the destruction of her cities. Their safety, it was said, hung upon the contingency of England aiding Poland. Canada is sure to be, as she has been, the battle-field of every war between Great Britain and the United States, and Canada must rely chiefly on her own arm for defence. Thus the strength of the enemy is wasted on battle-fields far distant from English shores. Those whose homes are in these happy and inaccessible islands, might form some conception of the dangers to which Canada is exposed, were it possible to reverse in imagination the condition of the two countries, by assuming that Canada was the head of the empire, and that England, with four millions of people, had France or some Power never her ally if not always her enemy, lying conterminous to her at every part of her boundary, and that boundary an imaginary line, a river or a lake; that in every war with Canada, 3,000 miles off, the legions from this kingdom of thirty millions would be poured over England's fair fields, to be followed by all the horrors of war in her homes and families. Again, let it be supposed that France was peopled with a kindred race, of the same language, religion, laws, and customs, and that union with her would save England from such dire consequences and secure her some portion of an almost fabulous prosperity; a prosperity, too, in great part the effect of Canadian capital and Canadian emigration. Further, let Englishmen see their French neighbours aspiring to and receiving the highest honours in the gift of a great nation, while they themselves were forced to be content with mere municipal honours. No, it is not interest that binds England's distant sons to the fatherland. There is no such cold calculation in their loyalty. It is that generous sentiment that leads a brother to prefer a brother's interests, to side with a brother against strangers, even when he knows he is wrong. An ardent affection is a jealous affection. It takes ill the rebuffs, the harsh criticisms, the cold calculating spirit with which aid is proffered, and the forgetfulness of all that is done and suffered in return. The sons of colonists enter the army and navy of England. A regiment is raised by one colony and others offered, but no mention is made of these when English statesmen and writers so often remind colonists that they keep amongst them a few soldiers, may be for Imperial purposes or for convenience; or, as after the Crimean war, 'because there were neither barracks nor other adequate accommodations in England.'

Britain in Europe stands in her island home a beacon-light, a teacher of constitutional liberty. Abroad, scattered over the face of the earth, are these co-workers with her—noble offshoots of a noble parent—labouring to consolidate constitutional governments amidst the anarchy of the new world, or in Africa on the borders of petty and degraded despotisms, or at the antipodes, where free scope is given over a broad continent for the development of British institutions. But not alone in their preferences for British institutions, nor in the promptness with which their sons have sprung to arms when England's honour or necessity called, not alone in the gift of a regiment to take their part with the soldiers of the empire, and in the educating so many of their sons for the army and navy of England,—has their affection for the land of their fathers been shown; but when, through famine, or war, or pestilence, the people of these islands have been in distress, by their domestic afflictions, have the hearts of Britons abroad been moved, and from every part of their broad lands contributions in food and money have flowed for the relief of the distressed in the old home. For the Irish famine of 1847, to make up the deficiency of scanty crops in Scotland, for the ⁎widows and orphans of Crimean soldiers, for the Lancashire operatives,—for all, Canada and Australia came forward as zealously as if the misery were at their own doors.

2. 'Does England draw her colonies, or her colonies draw her, into war? The colonies have the chief influence in Imperial implication in war. What brought us to the verge of hostilities on the Maine boundary, on the Musquito shore, or at San Juan's, or about the Newfoundland fisheries? or why are we now sending troops to Canada?' (*Mr. Adderley's Pamphlet*, p. 52.)

It would be a sufficient answer to these statements and questions that in none of the cases named was England involved in war, but that Canada has been drawn into two purely English quarrels; one in 1775, in sustaining the then tyrannical policy of the mother country; the other in 1812-15, when Europe in arms forced the dethroned Bourbons upon the French. In neither of which had Canada any interest, except that in the first the old colonies were fighting the battles of colonies, and in the second

France was asserting the right of a people to govern themselves.

'Why are we sending troops to Canada?' It would be trifling to attempt to show that the insult to the British flag, in the case of the Trent, did not arise in any way out of colonial interests. The 'Times,' too, as quoted by Mr. Adderley, asserted that, 'If Canada had not been a British possession, there would have been no reviling of England and no outrage committed on the English flag.' A previous question should have been asked and answered. Why do the United States show, and why have they always shown, such a want of amity towards England? Here lies the chief cause of the reviling and the outrages. Mark the treatment, too, that England received from Germany, and Prussia, and Austria, not to name Russia. Was all this because 'Canada was a British possession?' France has received from America, as well as from the German Powers, the most marked respect. She could trample the vaunted Munroe doctrine under the feet of her warriors, and erect an empire on the borders of the Great Republic; yet she and her citizens are treated with the utmost consideration, while it is painful to call to mind even a tithe of the indignities heaped upon British subjects and British shipping. As to the Maine boundary, the Musquito shore, and Newfoundland questions, they were settled in a very amicable way by the sacrifice of British territory and British interests.

Canada was in no way concerned in the San Juan question. But San Juan still remains, and no doubt many other occasions will be offered to the 'peace at any price' school to show their generosity in surrendering loyal British subjects, with their firesides, and their altars, and vast regions, to those who had foresworn their allegiance; only such cases must not be taken as a premium to revolt. Even after the fatted calf had been killed, and the old home made merry, was not all that remained the heir's? It is true the prodigal in this case was not restored, but what matter? Can we not still spin and weave for him? Wars may arise, and the difficulties of defence be increased by the surrender, but of what moment is this to Britain, if she no longer intends to defend her domain? In the meantime her peace is not disturbed, and she can buy and sell with the stranger as well as with her own household. Did not Rome, too, in her last days, for a time prevent war by the surrender of distant provinces?

America knows, Germany knows, that France will not submit to insults, and she receives none; and no doubt French policy, as a peace policy even, is safest. From England's peace policy grew the Russian war.

That the mother country is drawn into wars with

the aborigines in Africa and New Zealand are scarcely cases to be quoted in this connection, since for those settlements and the wars there the Government and Parliament of England are responsible. The enemy, too, are savages, and the wars local and exceptional. The natives are specially under the control of the Imperial authorities, and the colonists complain of the want of wisdom in such management. If England erects her flag in those countries, organizes a government, and sends them a governor, she does all these things with a full knowledge of all those questions of races involved in such a procedure. The old colonists now quoted as models had control of their own relations with the natives, and knew when to strike, and when to withhold the arm. Those who point the colonists of South Africa and New Zealand to the first settlers in America for examples, ought first, in all fairness, to make the conditions of the two the same; not place the one free and the other bound hand and foot in the forest amongst savages.

'It is even, in the nature of things, an impracticable system of government to let distant communities discuss their own policy, follow their own interests, make their own neighbour wars, and from the centre of the empire to undertake to maintain for them their various policy, protect their interests, and fight their wars.' (*Adderley*, p. 43.)

The entire colonial history of England is exactly the reverse of Mr. Adderley's statement. It is from the centre of the empire that wars are made, and the colonies are forced to fight, not their own, but England's wars—wars, too, usually, in which the colonists are involved against their own interests, wars originating in the injustice and folly of England, Englishmen themselves of all classes being the judges.

Earl Grey, in Mr. Mills' Committee, to a question (2622) relating to the war of 1812, 'that Canada did not pay towards raising troops,' replied, 'The danger to Canada during that war with the United States was entirely brought upon her by our most impolitic conduct towards the United States. Canada justly felt that she was only suffering from her connection with us.'

As to wars with native tribes, Mr. Adderley, with nearly all other members of Parliament and writers, forgets the facts—especially that the mother country manages the whole of the affairs with the aborigines—and Mr. Adderley has given us a sample of their administration in New Zealand; it is ' a simple confusion—an abomination.' Mr. Brodie, member for four years of the New Zealand Legislature, tells the Committee (*Ev.* 2874) that the control which the English Government retains over native affairs is the sole ground why England should pay for the troops in that colony—that the militia of New Zealand are a great deal better than the regular troops of the English army to deal with the natives—experience has proved that they are much more willing to follow the natives into the woods than the military—that the Executive of New Zealand have no control over the affairs of the natives.' (*See also Mr. Fitzgerald's Letter in 'Times,' June* 25, 1865.)

The colonists of the Cape of Good Hope have been as unjustly censured for the wars with the natives, because the blame seems to rest chiefly with the Home authorities—both the Home Government and the House of Commons—by first establishing the colonists in such a way as to expose them to be cut off singly by the natives, and then keeping the management of native affairs in Imperial hands. Earl Grey (*Ev.* 2557) states that 'the only two colonies exposed to attack by warlike natives are New Zealand and the Cape of Good Hope. In both I think the Government, and especially the House of Commons, must be taken to have encouraged colonization. The whole scheme of forming a settlement in the most exposed part of the Cape was originally brought forward by the Government, was sanctioned by the House of Commons, and was recommended particularly by those gentlemen in the House of Commons who were the great advocates for economy.

The Imperial Government not only founded the colony, but did so in a manner of all others most calculated to increase the danger and to diminish the power of the settlers to defend themselves. It placed single farm-houses over an extensive district, in situations in which they were utterly incapable of defending themselves. The Government at the same time took all the responsibility of defending the colony. The original settlers in North America were compact, and consequently capable of protecting themselves. In the absence of Imperial troops, I am persuaded a war of extermination would be carried on, ending in the destruction of the natives. A frightful amount of suffering to both parties would be endured in the meantime.' (*Ev.* 2559–2563.)

3. It is natural enough that a parent State should strive to shape the institutions of its dependencies after its own pattern. Whether it be monarchical Spain, France imperial or republican, or England, aristocratic and democratic so happily blended, each has set up its own institutions, civil and ecclesiastical, as the model. England for two centuries laboured in vain to establish an aristocracy and her State Church in her colonies. Spain had done the same before her. This has been a fruitful source of contention between the new and the old societies. A young and small community planted in a distant

land, and forced to govern itself, is democratic from necessity. The five settlers in Rhode Island, the 100 in Connecticut, the 120 pilgrims on Plymouth rock, in the 17th century, the small bands of Greek and Tyrian adventurers around the shores of the Mediterranean 3000 years ago, were voluntary associations and republics. In such communities there are no aristocracies and no peasants; universal suffrage at their origin is a necessity. That republics exist in America and despotisms in Asia, are proofs, the one of the youth, the other of the age of society, all due allowances being made for differences in the character and in the education, in its broadest sense, of the races of men that inhabit these two continents. Despotism superseded the republics on both shores of the Mediterranean, and feudal aristocracy in central Europe grew naturally out of the state of society— the warlike tribes with their chieftains. In British America, in Australia, in all such countries where lands are cheap, a peasant society similar to that of Europe cannot exist; the emigrant soon becomes the owner of land and as independent as any class of society. Nor can aristocracies in the European and Asiatic sense be created. Asia has her castes—the Brahmin, the soldier, merchant, and menial. None of these, not even as they are modified in European States, can exist as distinctive classes in those new countries. How, then, can the forms of government, the peculiar laws and usages, that have grown out of and been interwoven into the institutions of old communities, be forced upon new commonwealths, constituted so widely different? Changes must gradually supervene. The new and simple wants of young societies will give place to the more artificial forms and complicated interests of older communities; large manufacturing and commercial cities will rise up with turbulent populations; wars will create armies and a military class; modifications in the government would ensue; the executive arm would be strengthened to meet the new conditions of society, and to keep in check the rivalries and contentions of powerful parties and opposing interests.

4. Much angry comment has been wasted upon Canada during the American war, because she has not armed to meet the peculiar views of those large-minded members of Parliament and of the press, who have so kindly taken the affairs of all the world upon themselves, and relieved those distant and, because distant, benighted races from the trouble of thinking of their own concerns. The spirit and the matter of such strictures can have but one effect—that of creating a colonial in opposition to an Imperial party; of rendering more difficult the task of the friends of continued union in both countries, embittering the

connection while it lasts, and may be forcing an angry separation. All the world, too, had just been told by men in high positions in both Houses of Parliament, that 'all classes of Her Majesty's subjects in the North American provinces, had come forward and shown the determination at all hazards—and the hazards of war would in the first instance have fallen on themselves—to maintain their allegiance, and support the honour and dignity of the British Crown; and that this would be an important element in our future relations with the United States, and tend to secure us against the dangers of war with that country.' And again, that 'the Canadian people manifested an amount of energy and determination which has well merited the affection of the mother country.'

But the danger of war on the Trent affair soon passed away; and, in the opinions of Canadians—and events have thus far proved the correctness of those opinions—they were little likely to be molested during the civil war; they were, in fact, never safer.

Mr. Adderley may be taken as a representative of the more moderate class of writers on colonial affairs. In the preface to the new edition of his letter to Mr. Disraeli, he says:—

'Is Canada to be looked upon with satisfaction at this moment—is she safe, in the state of semi-dependency described in the following letter; free as to her government, legislation, and policy, but dependent upon English arms and funds for her defence and security? Is she likely to remain part of the British empire on an English guarantee of her liabilities; or to retain, on the credit of others, a fellow-citizenship the vital essence of which consists in self-defence?'

Mr. Adderley falls into the common habit of his countrymen of judging hastily and harshly of communities of which he can have little knowledge. If he is unacquainted with the present condition and character of the people of those provinces, and attaches no weight to the judgment of English statesmen, whose opinions had just been so freely expressed on the 'self-reliance' and 'determination of the Canadians to support the honour of the British Crown at all hazards—knowing that the hazards of war would in the first instance have fallen on themselves,' he ought not, at all events, to have ignored the entire history of that country, every event of which is directly at variance with the assertions here and in other parts of his pamphlet. In 1783, Upper Canada was settled by the loyalists, who had respected their oaths of allegiance, and fought the battles of monarchy against democracy, and of Britain against the old colonies. Chiefly by these very men, too, and their fathers, Canada had been conquered in 1759; and by the descendants of the same class defended, in 1812 and in 1837, with little assistance from the mother country. The unanimity and resolution shown to defend their own and British rights on the boundary question of 1846, brought by timid councils to such an inglorious end; the attitude assumed in 1861, when the flag of Britain had been insulted, an attitude which English statesmen declared prevented war; and the spirit displayed through the whole American war, and more especially called out at the close of this year (1864) to keep inviolate their soil; the entire history and present condition of those provinces, show that the assertions here and elsewhere as to the want of self-reliance of the Canadians and their dependence upon English arms, have no foundation, are, in fact, the pure inventions of the writers, if not the suggestions of pusillanimity, or of what Mr. Adderley styles 'supercilious ignorance.'

What more could be expected of any people? They have always successfully defended themselves, and against great odds and in wars brought on them by the folly of British statesmen.

In other places, Mr. Adderley, and writers of his class, equally draw upon their imaginations or their fears, when speaking of the British provinces falling voluntarily or from compulsion into the American

Republic. 'Let America only decompose,' says Mr. Adderley (p. xiv.), 'and reconstruct herself in the neighbourhood of Canada. There is no cohesion in the constitution of Canadian connection with England sufficient to resist the mere impact of any fragment from the ruins of the Union.'

Canada had defended herself for three years against the whole Union, when she was, compared with the States, far weaker than now. What power, then, would there be in the 'mere impact of any fragment,' to crush her? If Mr. Adderley's fears were suggested by the possible disintegration of the American Republic, and the formation in the North of a confederation free from slavery—that this new confederation, in having severed its connection from the slave-holding states, would have removed every or the chief objection of Canadians to a union with them—he knows little of the feelings or real opinions of the people of those provinces. The few who might be so influenced by such changed circumstances, would be chiefly those whose opinions were carried there with them. These, like those who went before them, modify their views, and their children, if they themselves do not, become what the educated classes there have long been, and now chiefly are in England, at the same time that they abhor slavery, and do their utmost to relieve the victims of it whenever they have the opportunity. Even England, with her strong sympathies on this subject, does not allow it to control her international relations. It made no difference in her intercourse with the United States when in union with the South, and while the Washington Government itself held slaves in the district of Columbia.

Slave-holding Turkey and Spain are the allies of Britain, and to uphold Turkey, England gave her blood and her treasures in the last war with Russia, as she had half a century before in support of Spain. The loyalty of the people of those provinces to their own country, and to the British Crown, their opinions of what their internal polity and their external relations ought to be, in no way depend on the question of a serf population in the Southern States, and the relation the North may sustain to them. In Mr. Mills' Committee, of which Mr. Adderley was a member, the Duke of Newcastle, while Colonial Minister, was asked this very question (*Ev.* 2989-90), ' whether he had ever considered the consequences of a confederation free from slavery, upon the political condition of Canada, and whether the mother country could rely upon the colony for her own defence under those changed circumstances?' His Grace declined to answer the questions, as being ' very speculative; he had considered them frequently, and all he could say was that, at the present moment, there is not a population more loyally disposed to the British Crown than the Canadian population. He spoke quite as much of the French as of the English.'

5. Mr. Adderley, at the close of his pamphlet, addressed to Mr. Disraeli, gives this summary of his object:—

'I hope I have given satisfactorily to your judgment, a fair comparison between our former and existing colonial system, and strong reasons for restoring the former.'

One part of that former system was, as we are informed by Mr. Adderley, and those who think with him, that the old colonists made war in Canada, Nova Scotia, and Cape Breton, upon the Indian tribes, and even in the West Indies. Modern colonists have adopted a different policy, and tried to live peaceably by the side of their neighbours. Canada, says Mr. Adderley, has not fully regained the ancient type. Hence the inference that her people are made of less stern stuff than the more quarrelsome race of former generations. This is to look at but half the question.

Take, as an example, the British provinces which have grown up by the side of the old colonies, and we shall find that they have as bravely and successfully defended themselves from both Indian tribes and foreign enemies, as those earlier pioneers, with whom it is now the fashion to compare or contrast them. They have kept the peace with their neighbours, and protected their country from all invasions. They have never involved the parent State in war, but have freely given their blood in defence of themselves and the empire, when drawn into the quarrels of England, on even a policy now strongly condemned by English statesmen.

After some very flattering compliments to these provinces, Mr. Adderley adds, 'Canada still wants the corollary of self-government—self-defence.'

It is difficult to understand the ideas attached by these writers to 'self-defence,' unless it be explained by Mr. Adderley's reviewer ('Times,' January 23, 1863), who seems to put his whole meaning, not in a postscript indeed, but in his last sentence. 'We are not inviting Canada to emulate our ancient colonists, and present Maine to the mother country as a testimony of their prowess.'

If Canada had any such ambition to emulate the ancient type, she would probably remember that her militia did conquer Michigan, a state even larger than Maine, and larger than England, with several forts on her frontier, in the war in 1812, and 'presented them to the mother country,' but they were very condescendingly taken from her loyal children and presented again to the descendants of the old type of rebels. Maine, too, thirty years afterwards, with her loyal British population, was turned over to the Republic, because the Republic demanded it. What guarantee would Canada have in thus showing her prowess that the prize would be retained?

The warlike propensities of the old colonists cannot be referred to as proof of their higher spirit. There is, no doubt, as high a tone of feeling amongst Englishmen and Frenchmen at the present day, as when they were more demonstrative in showing it; but there may be a higher morality, a better appreciation of international duties. The one is the passion of the boy, the other the maturer wisdom of the man. Do those who now laud the spirit of the old colonies, approve their war policy? Does not the spirit of the colonists more correctly represent that of the mother country at the present day, living at peace with their neighbours, unless when forced to draw the sword in self-defence?

'It would be unjust to say the military spirit is wanting in Canada. I do not know that Canada has done, or omitted to do, anything otherwise than might fairly have been expected under the circumstances. There was a higher tone of feeling in the old colonies, arising from passion and hatred between England

and France, such as I would not wish to see between Canada and the United States.' (*Gladstone's Evidence*, 3842-5.)

6. 'The cost of our colonies to the British exchequer is a question which has only recently disquieted us. There was a time when we attempted to tax our colonies at our discretion, and now we enable them to tax us—they claim the control of our resources now. We allow Canada to appropriate its clergy reserves, and we assist Canada to pay its archdeacons. We pay for driving Chinese out of the way of Australian diggers. We pay £40,000 a year for the police expenses in the West Indies, and £15,000 for the maintenance of pest holes on the coast of West Africa. We pay still more for the difficulties of the New Zealand colonies, with their Maories. We pay £27,000 to the Cape for improving the Caffres, and £400,000 a year for shooting them. We pay for the nucleus of protection in nearly all the colonies, which deters the colonists from initiating protection for themselves.' (*Review of Mr. Adderley's Pamphlet*, 'Times,' January 23, 1863.)

We have here the chief items of the indictment brought against the colonies by Mr. Adderley, and reiterated by those who have not Mr. Adderley's candour nor his knowledge of the subject. Part of them the colonies proper have nothing to do with. If the Imperial government choose to bear the police expenses of the West Indies, to keep up 'pest holes' on the west coast of Africa, 'where all life dies and all death lives,' to support archdeacons in a country which will not tolerate a State-paid clergy, to pay £27,000 a year to improve the Caffres, and then £400,000 a year to shoot them,—these and similar question we suppose are matters of taste, or mysteries of the colonial office. If, moreover, British statesmen find it convenient to fight their political battles on such questions, none can find fault with them; but it is ungenerous and unjust to charge the folly of the Imperial policy upon the colonists, and stupid to confound the cost of garrisons and naval stations, and the expenses connected with forty posts and dependencies, with those colonies that have nothing in the world to do with them. England for her own interests, real or imaginary, expends a million and a half sterling on garrisons, convict settlements, and stations connected with her anti-slavery policy, and another million and more on islands in the East and West Indies, portions of South Africa, Kaffraria, Natal, &c. peopled in whole or part by native races. Why should these be confounded with those great communities of Englishmen in North America and Australia, whose trade with the mother country sums up to £35,000,000 a year, but yet against which we find in the Committee's Report only some £630,000 cost to the British exchequer, and out of even this must be taken at all events the amount of expenses for purely Imperial purposes at Halifax if not at Quebec, and for troops, too, when kept in Canada, as the Duke of Newcastle (*Ev.* 2452) and Earl Grey (*Ev.* 2620) state because they are better off there, or because there were neither barracks nor other accommodations in England.

A little attention to the circumstances connected with the cases referred to would have saved these writers from the inaccuracies into which they have fallen, and which do great injustice to our fellow-subjects, often struggling for existence itself in those young and sparsely settled countries. If every man in England capable of bearing arms were called upon for the defence of his fireside, we should have a better idea of the sacrifices which the colonists in New Zealand and in South Africa have made. When we add to this the responsibility of the Government and Parliament in founding those settlements in a manner the most exposed to attack from the natives, and in positions where mutual support was utterly impossible, and that the Home Government reserved to itself all control over the relations between the colonists and natives, we shall have a very fair example of the thoughtless and ungenerous strictures which embitter the minds of those at first genuinely loyal subjects, and raise up a colonial in opposition to an Imperial party. The effect of such language, whether in the press or in Parliament, is only evil.

The colonists maintain that the war (New Zealand) is an Imperial one, undertaken by Imperial officers, on Imperial grounds, cheerfully and generously aided by the colonists at a cost of which England has little conception—every man from fifteen to fifty-five being under arms. In September 1861, the first wholly responsible government was formed, and Sir George Grey then (1861) agreed to act by the advice of his ministry in native affairs—now (1864) he has taken those affairs into his own hands. The colonists are indignant at the accusations in Parliament and in the press, that they encourage the war on account of the Imperial expenditure, and the general unjust strictures in England upon them in the midst of their great sufferings brought on them by English policy. (*Correspondence of Times*, December 15; New Zealand, October 14, 1864; also *Times*, January 25, 1865.)

Earl Grey in his evidence (2557–2563) before the Select Committee of 1861, gives a somewhat explicit account of the origin and nature of these settlements.

The only two colonies, he informs us, exposed to attack from warlike natives are New Zealand and the Cape of Good Hope, in both of which the Government, and more particularly the House of Commons, encouraged the colonization, more especially to the Cape; the whole scheme of forming settlements in the most exposed parts was originally brought forward by the Government, sanctioned by the House of Commons, and recommended particularly by the great advocates of economy in the House of Commons, as Mr. Hume. 'The Imperial Government not only founded the colony, but did so in a manner of all others most calculated to increase the danger and diminish the power of the settlers to defend themselves, by placing single farm-houses over an extensive district, in exposed situations. The Government at the same time took the responsibility of defending the colony.' The original settlers in North America left to themselves were compact, giving each other support.

Equally unjust are the complaints that England pays archdeacons and clergy in Canada; for Canada has no archdeacons or clergy in the sense here understood. She has no Established Church. The Crown, in pursuance of the policy of transplanting her ecclesiastical system in the colonies, assumed the responsibility of paying certain clergy whom they sent there : but the Canadian Government have no such responsibility, and no Canadian ministry could stand a day who should advocate such a policy, or who should assume the responsibility of paying the clergy. The clergy reserves were the lands of the province, made valuable by the labour of its inhabitants, and were hence thrown into the public exchequer for the benefit of all, strict faith being kept with those clergymen who were in receipt of anything from that fund.

7. In the opinions of Englishmen of three generations the old colonists were driven from their allegiance by the most unaccountable blunders of the statesmen of that day. After much opposition, constitutional government has at length been granted to the more important dependencies of the empire, and the justice of their demands thus admitted. The attempts to incorporate the ecclesiastical with the civil power in the colonies were miserable failures. On these and other important questions, succeeding generations have admitted that the colonists were right, which is only to admit that they are the best judges of their own circumstances, and best qualified to manage their own affairs. Whether they have free-trade or protection; whether a revenue should be raised by direct or indirect taxation in the colonies; whether those great countries are to be deprived of all control over their

foreign relations, and drawn or driven by a power not their own into war, reduced to the condition of municipalities, and without the right of even a municipality to be represented in the councils of the empire; whether Australia should admit convicts to any part of that continent to contaminate their population, to stain their good name, and add vastly to their police expenditure: on all such questions no Englishman can doubt that the colonists are thoroughly in earnest, and, whatever may be thought of the justice of their case, the history of the past cannot but suggest moderation in the views of Imperial statesmen.

8. Imperial interests in the colonies are represented by a governor appointed by the Crown; to him is given the power of disallowing acts of the colonial legislature, and the same power is reserved to the Crown. The governor is instructed to be specially watchful over questions affecting the mother country; his personal influence is much relied on in guiding legislation. Despatches, too, from the Minister of State, and less frequently the outlines of bills, are added to all the other agencies used to mould colonial action in accordance with Imperial interests, real or imaginary. Over and above all this, Parliament reserves the right to legislate for every part of the empire; the proclamations of the sovereign and the

orders of the home courts may have the same force in the remotest dependency as in the United Kingdom. In several of the colonies, moreover, the second chamber is appointed by the Crown. But have colonists no reciprocal interests in the legislation of Parliament and in the action of the Imperial authorities? Colonial representation in Parliament, it is said, is an impossibility—at all events, inadmissible. The smallest States, not larger than a colonial municipality, accredit ministers or agents to all countries where their interests are of sufficient importance. The ministers of the United States at all the courts, and their consuls at the ports of every nation of Europe, have had a powerful influence in directing to their shores the four millions of emigrants from 1800 to 1865 who have gone from the United Kingdom, and the many more millions from Europe, to that Republic instead of to British colonies.

9. 'It is inexpedient that the proportion of cost of colonial defence to be borne by the Imperial and colonial governments respectively should be the subject of negotiations with the various dependencies, but that evidence has been given tending to show that the policy successfully adopted by Lord Grey in 1851, in announcing to the free Australian colonies the terms on which alone Imperial troops could be sent there, may be gradually extended to other

dependencies possessing responsible government.' (*Report of the Select Committee of the House of Commons on Col. Mil. Ex.* 1861.)

'I have always said I would advise the policy adopted by Earl Grey in 1851 towards the Australian colonies'—announcing to the colonists the Imperial policy without consulting them. (*Mr. Godley's Evidence,* 2198.)

'The assistance of England should be only in the shape of contribution—one half—and one half would be a fair compromise. (*Mr. Godley's Evidence,* 2176, 2192.) 'The assistance not to vary with the danger.' (2193.) 'The existence upon the frontier of Canada of a first-class Power, with which Canada is liable to be involved in war, not by her own act but by the policy of the Home Government, should be no element in calculating the assistance to be offered Canada.' (2194.)

Such opinions as these last carry their own refutation with them. Happily they have found little favour amongst the ruling minds at the Colonial Office.

Mr. Merivale's evidence on this point may be set off against the above.

'The colonies are of such entirely different classes that I feel it impossible to apply any uniform rule to the question of what proportion of their defence the mother country ought to contribute. There are cases in which England had better assume the whole defence.' (2211.) 'The colonies in West Africa are kept up for Imperial purposes, and in the case of the North American colonies it is an extremely difficult question whether you should call contributions from the colonies, or to what extent, although I am not prepared to say that you should not do so.' (2221.) 'In Newfoundland you have the disagreeable task of watching the execution of treaties. In Nova Scotia you have one of the most important military stations which you possess. Canada is a great country, and all our relations with Canada are the relations of one great country with another. No ordinary colonial principles apply.'

So the Duke of Newcastle, on a question of colonial policy somewhat similar, says in his evidence (2946):—

'I differ from the position assumed throughout that letter (*General Peel's*), namely, *that one rigid rule can be applied to the whole of the colonies of the empire.* I think that to be an entire folly—a theory which will not bear examination, nor can it be carried into practice.'

Earl Grey, too, is equally explicit in condemning a policy founded on one rigid rule in its application to fifty colonies, differing almost as widely as any fifty independent communities possibly can. 'Garrisons, as Gibraltar, Malta, and Halifax, are held for our general naval purposes. A different rule must be applied to these. The Australian colonies are a peculiar case; there are no native tribes, and little danger from foreign enemies. The Government and Parliament are responsible for the peculiar settlements at the Cape and in New Zealand, and took at the same time all the responsibility of defending them.' (*Evidence*, 2530-3, 2557-60.)

Yet Earl Grey is a strong advocate for authority on the one side and obedience on the other, and when Secretary for the Colonies, in Earl Russell's Government, in his famous despatches in reference to the press of Canada, resorted to the style of argument of Jupiter in the fable with the countryman— first reasoned, then threatened the thunderbolts of the empire against those who refused to be convinced.

10. 'I have already related the answer of Virginia to James I., even in the hour of peril, refusing to receive English troops on any other terms, unless placed under the control of their own governor, and paid by the votes of their own Assembly. It is certain that the old colonies would have insisted on this last condition as essential to their rights [safety?]. If the sight of English red-coats at all times has become a needful support of Canadian confidence, and English pay has ceased to be resented as a symptom of de-

pendence, we must bow humbly under the conviction that Canada is no longer inhabited by men like those who conquered her. Even in 1812 she needed no nucleus around which to organize a powerful militia, though then the ancient colonial spirit was so far changed that she permitted England to furnish her militia with arms and pay.'

Mr. Adderley, who represents one class of English statesmen and writers, very conveniently leaves out of sight the entire history of Canada except the incidental reference to that of 1812. He might have remembered that Canada, in 1783, was settled by the very men and their sons who composed the chief force in its conquest twenty-four years before: thus it was the conquerors who occupied it; and that in 1812 their descendants defended it against vast odds. In 1837 they saved it against Yankee fillibusters, and an internal rebellion brought on by English misgovernment. The insult to an English ship in 1861 filled them with the same indignation as animated their fellow-subjects at home, and showed that they were ready to suffer all the hazards and horrors of war in defence of that flag under the protection of which their forefathers had taken possession of their fair land. Canada has defended herself against every attack, and more successfully than our brave old forefathers did in days of yore, when they found it

M

more convenient to fraternize with the conqueror than to expel the invader. Canada, it may be, does not quake as often as the timid in the dear old isle are frightened from their propriety, and this comes periodically. If a hue and cry is got up every night after a 'Zouave in the Premier's wardrobe,' why should not a Yankee be looked for in the Governor-General's? England wished Canada to turn out a militia force equal to 1,200,000 for the mother country, merely to play the soldier after Canada knew there was no danger.

Mr. Adderley refers to the reply of the Virginians to James I., refusing to receive the English troops, 'unless placed under the *control* of their own *governor* and paid by the votes of their own Assembly,' as a proof of their high spirit in contrast with that of colonists of the present day. If Mr. Adderley had forgotten other facts in the history of the old colonists which place such acts on an entirely different ground, the one he here quotes, and the terms used in describing it, ought to have saved him from attributing it to considerations nowhere expressed, and especially from drawing inferences so ungenerous— inferences applicable to any people on the globe more than to those whom he censures—a people who have in so *short a period* created for themselves a country —a nation, surpassing in population and wealth three-fourths of the States of Europe, who have from the beginning till now defended their country against a powerful enemy, and have effected, often against the strong opposition of the Imperial authorities, the most important changes in their constitution and internal polity, as the Union Act of 1841, responsible government, election of the Legislative Council, the final settlement of the clergy reserve and rectory questions, and the Seigniorial Tenure Bill; the latter of itself accomplishing a great social revolution which could find its counterpart in Europe only in having the feudal system of France of the sixteenth century swept away peacefully by legislative acts. These were all, when left to the local legislatures, effected without disturbing for a day the peace of the community.

Virginia demanded that the troops should be ' placed under the control of her *own* governor, and paid by their own legislature.' The military would then be subject to the civil authorities of the colony, and not to a Power suspected of trying to wrest from them their liberties. Light is thrown upon this by other events in the history of those colonies. When, in 1772, the British Government determined that the Governor of Massachusetts should be paid by the Crown, ' the representatives of Massachusetts passed resolutions expressing great dissatisfaction with the new regulations of the British Government by which the Governor was to have his support from the Crown.' They declared it to be an infraction of their charter. They pointed out the *evils that would result from the measure*, by which the Governor would be rendered independent of the people, of whose interests and liberties he was designed to be the public guardian.' (*Holmes' An.* 1779.)

Here it is fear of losing their liberties, and not high spirit or generosity, which makes them demand the right to pay their own governor.

So, when, in 1641, Massachusetts sent a deputation to England 'to give, amongst many other things, her creditors satisfaction, they were advised to ask for Parliamentary aid; the reason assigned for not following that advice is very remarkable. That reason was, the apprehension of subjection to Parliament.' (*Holmes' An.* 1641.)

Here, again, it is neither generosity nor high spirit, but fear, mistrust, which actuates the colonists.

And in their attempts to conquer Nova Scotia and Canada, the colonists were not assisted by England, because England feared the too rapid growth of her vigorous and virtually independent offshoots, and rather discouraged than aided them.

Those colonies, too, regarded themselves as independent of the Parliament of England, and so acted from the beginning; and when the struggle came for dominion by the Imperial legislature over those States, it was the struggle between a powerful nation on the one hand and weak yet independent ones on the other. The colonies never submitted to Parliament, and Parliament could never enforce obedience. Finally, although at one time they acknowledged 'Parliament as the supreme legislature of the whole empire,' after the passage of the Stamp Act in 1765 they disputed it, and in the Declaration of Independence, make no mention of Parliament, but treat the acts of oppression there named as acts of the King in combination 'with others' for the overthrow of their liberties.

CHAPTER X.

EVIDENCE GIVEN BEFORE THE SELECT COMMITTEE OF THE HOUSE OF COMMONS ON COLONIAL MILITARY EXPENDITURE IN 1861.

Evidence before Select Committee, 1861—Duke of Newcastle—Mr. Merivale—Lord Herbert—General Burgoyne—Mr. Gladstone—Earl Grey—Mr. Godley—Mr. Brodie—Mr. Elliot—Mr. Lowe. Pp. 166–194.

I. *Extracts from the Evidence of* THE DUKE OF NEWCASTLE, *Secretary of State for the Colonies, also Secretary of State for War and the Colonies in* 1853.

Evidence 2945. Do you concur in the opinion of General Peel, that England should assist in the defence of her colonies against aggression on the part of foreign civilised nations, and in less proportion of formidable native tribes, but in no case except when such colonies are mere garrisons kept up for Imperial purposes should she assume the whole of such defence?—No; I think it is a theory which looks extremely well on paper, but I do not think it is one which will well bear minute examination, or which can be carried into practice. (2946.) *I differ from the position which is assumed throughout that letter, namely, that one rigid rule can be applied to the whole of the colonies of the empire.* I think that to be an entire folly.

2952. In 1856 five regiments were stationed in the North American colonies, three in Canada (after having been reduced to one before the Russian war), probably on account of apprehended difficulty with the United States, arising out of the recruitment question, *or matter of convenience,* for which there were neither barracks nor other adequate accommodations in this country. I only give an answer as wishing to imply that it was occasioned more by motives of Imperial policy than either at the demand or for the requirements of the colony. (2955.) You (the Committee) have stated the number of Imperial forces as considerably higher than it now stands. Your returns are, I think, for 1858-9. Now they are 2,220. One object (2956) of the troops being kept in Canada is for defence from foreign aggression. (2957.) The frontier line is 3,000 miles. (2960.) The total cost of defence for the year 1859, in Nova Scotia and Newfoundland, was £170,000.

2961. The revenue of Nova Scotia is £300,000 a year. Halifax is not kept up for the benefit of

Nova Scotia. I look upon it much as if you were to say that because Portsmouth is in the county of Hampshire, Hampshire should be called upon to pay for the expenses of the garrison of Portsmouth. Halifax is an important military post; it is still more important as a naval station; it is one of the finest, and, in all probability, the finest harbour in the world. Halifax should no more be supported by Nova Scotia, than Portsmouth by Hampshire. (3021.) [*By the Committee.*] Would it be fair, then, to impose upon Nova Scotia its share of the expenses of the Imperial fort at Halifax, as Hampshire bears its full share of the cost of the defence of England? —Perfectly fair. It is extremely difficult to argue these questions upon principles of business, and it is a very small ground to take. It might relieve that expense by some few pounds. It would be a very pettifogging and weak argument. (3023.) Bermuda and Halifax are so dissimilar, that I cannot look upon the one as an equivalent for the other in any respect whatever. Bermuda is a very bad naval station; it is a military post kept up for military purposes; the ships which can get into Bermuda are very small ones; a first-rate ship of the line can hardly get into Bermuda. Halifax is a great naval station; all the navies in the world can be sheltered in it. You might fight a naval engagement in Bedford basin. Then there are two other basins.

3045. Do you consider it any sufficient reason why Canada should not contribute to the military expenditure for her defence because of the agreement with the Imperial Government?—Canada and Australia are differently situated. Canadians say that if they are involved in war it is by act of the mother country, and with the United States in some such question as the San Juan, or the recruitment dispute, with reference to the army in the Crimea; we shall suffer enough then. That is the way in which they argue.

2968. Do you think that a federal union of the North American provinces would tend to facilitate the arrangement for the more efficient and economical defence of those provinces?—That is a very important political question, and I am rather disinclined to answer it in any sense which would imply, on my part, before a committee of this character, the advocacy of a federal union. Various schemes have been proposed, some for a federal union, some for a legislative union; and it is a question which has been much discussed, and in which opposing interests in Canada and the Lower Provinces are naturally involved; and I would rather not answer the question except to this extent—that, of course, any plan which throws the government of all those countries into one united Power, would facilitate arrangements for the construction of railways.

2982. Ten thousand volunteers and militia in British North America would not represent one tenth of those who would come forward upon occasion. Whenever there has been any threat of war, the colonists have invariably shown the best spirit, and the greatest readiness to come forward and assist the Imperial Government. When they have roads and other works to construct which exhaust all their available resources, they are unwilling to pay large sums out of their small revenues for military purposes in time of peace.

2986. Colonies are not in a position to provide by volunteers a force for forts like Quebec and Halifax.

2989. Have you ever considered the consequences of a confederation free from slavery, upon the political condition and political opinions of Canada?—I have considered it very frequently. 2990. Could we under these changed circumstances, depend upon the colony for its own defence?—These are speculative questions; all I can say is, that I believe that at the present moment there is not a population more loyally disposed to the British Crown than the Canadian population. I speak quite as much of the

French population as of the English. (2292.) One of the duties which devolve upon the mother country is the defence of a colony. Canada stands in a different position from any other colony. The real defence of Australia must be our fleet; but the fleet can do little to defend Canada.

2997. I cannot allow by any means that Canada is now simply a cost to this country. Without entering into the discussion, I must be excused if I do not, by my silence, admit the position that they have excluded English goods by their legislation. That their tariff is higher than, either for their own sakes or for English manufactures, would be desirable, I admit, but I do not think that it has been imposed for protection purposes, but on account of the financial position of the country.

3009. [*By Mr. Adderley.*] I understand your Grace to say that the only remaining feature of dependence in Canada upon England is the distinction of Imperial garrisons?—I do not think I said the only; what I intended to say was, that I thought the distinction between a colony and an independent country, if you withdraw all notion of defending it, would become infinitesimal. (3010.) It is not a question of colonial dependence, but a question of colonial empire. I believe that the retention of our colonial empire is of importance to us.

II. *Extracts from the Evidence of* HERMAN MERIVALE, C.B., *Under-Secretary for the Colonies from* 1847 *to* 1860.

2210. The colonies are of such entirely different classes, that I feel it impossible to apply any uniform rule to the question of what proportion of their defence the mother country ought to contribute. There are cases in which England had better assume the whole defence. (2211.) The colonies in West Africa are kept up for Imperial purposes, and in the case of the North American colonies, where the object in maintaining a force is a political and not a colonial object, it is an extremely difficult question whether you should call contributions from the colony, or to what extent, although I am not prepared to say that you should not do so. (2221-2.) In Newfoundland you have the disagreeable task of watching the execution of treaties. In Nova Scotia you have one of the most important military stations which you possess. Canada is a great country, and all our relations with Canada are the relations of one great country with another. No ordinary colonial principles apply.

2227. Lord Grey originated the idea of a colonial railway to go from Halifax to Quebec: he was willing that this country should contribute.

2241. I never heard that the arrangement of

Earl Grey produced any dissatisfaction in Australia. [Earl Grey announced to the Australian colonists, without any previous understanding with them, the conditions on which the Imperial Government would give assistance in defence.]

2243. The Australian colonies have no permanent apprehension or idea of foreign Powers or invasion. In Canada it is always present. They consider that the business of this country is to take care of them in the event of political complications of which they are not in any way the cause, and of which they expect they will be the victims. (2245.) Canada would be in the first instance the battle-field in their opinion.

2261. There is a great difference between a purely English community, like New Brunswick and Nova Scotia, and a mixed and foreign community like the West Indies.

2262. We maintain troops in colonies: 1, By way of insurance against foreign aggression; 2, insurance against internal disturbance; and 3, against danger from native tribes. (2287.) The case between Canada and this country raises a different question from that between this country and Nova Scotia. It is a question between nations—for England and Canada are nations.

2390. I think if the North American colonies do

federate or amalgamate, it will in all probability render the slight tie that still subsists between them and us somewhat slighter; in that case the probability is that it will not be deemed necessary to maintain troops there any longer. (*See Duke of Newcastle's Ev.* 3045.) (2392.) If their foreign policy still remain with England, you must maintain troops.

2457. I look upon the occupation of Vancouver's Island as simply an Imperial object with which the interest of Canada is not implicated. I cannot see the slightest interest that Canada had in the question.

2521. Do you not see your way clear in laying down any uniform system as a guide for the Imperial Government in dealing with the military expenditure of the various colonies?—I do not.

2522. Do you think that the want of such an uniform system has been felt as a serious evil?—No, I think it an evil of administration, but nothing more. (2524.) I do not consider it a system at all. (2525.) When Lord Grey wrote the despatch to the Australian colonies in 1851, responsible government had not been given. We then did comparatively as we liked with the revenues and executive administration of the Australian colonies. Lord Grey was not fettered with that difficulty in laying down his principle which would exist now. (2526.) There are no colonies now of any consequence in the same position as the Australian colonies were then.

2496. I do not think you could draw any conclusion from one colony to another [referring to Lord Grey's rule, number 11, Report Sel. Com.]

2516–17. Are you prepared to hand over to the colonial authorities the whole native policy, unless you can at the same time call upon them to supply the whole cost of any military operations to which that policy may lead?—I think so. I admit it is a choice of evils; but supposing that we are compelled to keep the troops there, I think, on the whole, the colony would be better managed if there were no limits as regards native affairs.

2346–2350. The trade of Australia is forty millions. Almost the whole of that property, when at sea and in the harbours, is British property. The interest which the colonies have in it while on board ship is very small indeed. British property is entirely insured at home. (2350.) [These friendly harbours and waters give great protection to such British property without the presence of a naval force so necessary in other countries.]

III. *Extracts from the Evidence of* Lord Herbert, *Secretary of State for War.*

3637. [*By the Committee.*] You stated that Canada lying conterminous with a powerful State, is a colony in which we should retain a nucleus of force in case of hostile operations. Mr. Lowe (3371) gave it as his opinion that the greater the exposure of the colony to such danger the greater was the necessity for making the colony self-reliant?—I think that is an extreme view of the question.

3638. Mr. Lowe (3405) gave it as his opinion that for every soldier we sent to such a colony as Canada we prevented a hundred colonists from taking up arms; do you take the same view?—It is impossible for me to say upon what data that opinion is founded. (3641.) A small force would be a nucleus around which the colonists would rally, and which would assist them in their military organization. (*Earl Grey's Ev.* 2621.)

3641. Mr. Lowe stated that he would have no Imperial troops in any colony in time of peace, but only in case of war?—My opinion is the reverse of that. (3648.) I do not see that sending troops to the colonies has inflicted upon us the necessity of having mercenaries in time of war.

3501. Whenever there is an Imperial necessity to

concentrate troops on one point, the rest of the colonies are starved, without reference to their wants at the time. In the Russian war we denuded the colonies of troops.

3512. I think you may look forward to the time when the necessity for sending troops to Canada may cease, or, at all events, be greatly diminished. (3511.) They have now a considerable force of volunteers.

2529. The total cost of transport to and from the colonies, including garrisons, fortresses, &c. amounted in 1859 to £200,000.

3546–7. Sir William Denison, in his despatches, August 1856, has recommended that a colony should be left to bear the primary responsibility of its defence, and that the mother country should only assist. The principle therein enunciated is certainly to be arrived at.

IV. *Extracts from the Evidence of General* SIR J. F. BURGOYNE, *Inspector-General of Fortifications.*

1301. England bases all her calculations upon the assumption that she will be permanently in possession of the sea.

1254. We ought to maintain in strength, besides Mediterranean garrisons, principally Mauritius, Bermuda (1339), Kingston, Quebec, and Halifax; and secondarily, the Cape, Ceylon, Hong-Kong, and St. Helena; and for coaling stations (1254), Aden, Seychelles, and the Falkland Islands (1313). £26,000 have been voted for a citadel at Halifax. This vote was on a calculation made twenty years ago, and is not sufficient.

1336. The presence of British troops discourages local efforts for defence. [See Lord Herbert's evidence, 3638 and 3641.] (1330, 1351.) If the colonists are indifferent, our garrisons could not defend Halifax or Canada.

1356. In reference to the analogy referred to by Mr. Godley (2070, 2072, 2195) between the old American colonies and those of the present day, General Burgoyne says, 'The colonial troops which conquered Halifax, Nova Scotia, and Cape Breton, were ten to one in force to the regulars opposed to them.' [If Canada were ten to one to the United States, instead of being one to ten, she would require no assistance.]

1358. The old colonists garrisoned the principal places, but it was against a very small body of troops.

1365. We now incur very trifling expenses for the fortifications of Kingston and Quebec—just for small repairs and maintenance.

V. *Extracts from the Evidence of* THE RIGHT HON. W. E. GLADSTONE, *Chancellor of the Exchequer.*

3838. The obligation of the mother country cannot be overlooked, and I do not say she is not bound to defend her colonies; but what I venture to say is, that the system under which the colonial community itself is primarily charged with the duty of her own defence, is by far the best, both for the mother country and the colony—such a system as did exist in the case of the old American colonies. (3783.) [*By the Committee.*] Were they not in fact independent States, and did we not take possession of them?—I do not think the old American colonies, previous to the revolution, were independent States any further, or in any other sense, than in a sense in which it is extremely desirable that all our principal colonies should be independent States.

3785. I should say these colonies were in a state of much less independence than Canada is now, because it would not have been permitted to them to legislate adversely to the mother country, as in the case of the North American colonies.

3842. It would be unjust to say the military spirit is wanting in Canada. I do not know that Canada has done or omitted to do anything otherwise than might fairly have been expected under the circumstances. There was a higher tone of feeling in the old colonies (3844), arising from passion and hatred between England and France (3845), such as I would not wish to see between Canada and the United States.

3768. The greatest difficulty attached to the subject of our colonial military expenditure, is the uninformed and immature, and generally indifferent state of public opinion upon it in this country.

3780. To arrive at a system under which the primary responsibility of self-defence by land should be thrown on the colonists themselves would be not only an immense advantage to the British exchequer, but would have many still more important and higher recommendations, independently of the question of cost [which to colonies proper, not military and naval stations, amounts to only some three-quarters of one million sterling.]

3787. The really valuable tie with a colony is the moral and social tie. If the feelings of Canada are not with us, I do not think she will remain with us because we charge ourselves with the burden of her defence.

3797. In proportion as responsibilities are accepted by colonial communities, they will be more disposed to go beyond the bare idea of self-defence, and to render loyal and effective assistance in the struggles of empire.

3798. As regards colonies generally, while England has supremacy at sea, they are safe [of British America what?], and the fortifications and colonial garrisons in the West Indies, and many others, are little, if at all, required. If England has not supremacy at sea, you are only making victims of those garrisons.

3834. I should like to see the *state of feeling* restored to the colonies which induced the first American colonists to make it one of their grievances that British troops were kept in their borders *without their consent*. [That feeling was mistrust of the Crown and of her troops, the same as existed in England in the Parliamentary party. Hence the objection of the colonists to the troops without their consent and when not under their control.]

VI.—*Extracts from the Evidence of* EARL GREY.

2531. I cannot conceive how you can hold colonies without acknowledging the obligation, within certain limits, to protect them. (2532.) For a long series of years this country has acted on the principle of taking their defence entirely upon herself.

The introduction of a different principle requires great caution.

2529. The colonists ought to undertake to provide for the expense of barracks for such of Her Majesty's troops as may be stationed in them for their protection. (2530.) A different rule must be applied to those stations which are supported as garrisons for the general purposes of the empire. I refer to such places as Gibraltar and Malta. (2543.) The fortress of Halifax is to be looked at as a place of the same character as Malta or Gibraltar, of which the possession is of importance with a view to our general naval power.

2531. [*By the Committee.*] So the main ground upon which, in your opinion, the claim of those colonies not classed as military stations, to Imperial aid in their defence, is the risk they run in being involved in the wars of England with other Powers?—I should hardly say that: I think that the very notion of a colonial relation implies protection on the one side and obedience on the other, within certain limits. I cannot conceive how you can hold colonies without acknowledging the obligation, within certain limits, to protect them. (2533.) The Australian colonies are certainly a peculiar case; they are infinitely less exposed to the attacks of any foreign enemy than any other portions of the British dominions, and there are no native tribes from whom the slightest danger can be apprehended. (2557.) The only two colonies exposed to attack by warlike natives are New Zealand and the Cape of Good Hope; in both, I think, the Government, and especially the House of Commons, must be taken to have encouraged colonization, more particularly to the Cape. The whole scheme of forming a settlement in the most exposed part of the Cape was originally brought forward by the Government, was sanctioned by the House of Commons, and was recommended, particularly by those gentlemen in the House of Commons who were then the great advocates for economy. Mr. Hume was one of the principal promoters of the settlement of Albany (in 1819). (2559.) A great responsibility attaches to the Imperial Government in reference to the defence of the colony; the Imperial Government not only founded the colony, but did so in a manner of all others most calculated to increase the danger, and to diminish the power of the settlers to defend themselves. It placed single farm-houses over an extensive district, in situations in which they were utterly incapable of defending themselves. (2560.) The Government, at the same time, took all the responsibility of defending the colony. The original settlements in North America were compact, and the settlers were consequently capable of protecting themselves.

2563. In the absence of Imperial troops, I am persuaded that both in New Zealand and at the Cape a war of extermination would be carried on. It would probably end in the destruction of the native races. A frightful amount of suffering to both parties would be endured in the meantime. (2581.) Whether colonies (as New Zealand and the Cape) should furnish local troops or contribute towards the maintenance of Imperial troops, must depend upon the circumstances of the colony. It is frequently extremely unadvisable to require them to furnish local troops, because labour is so excessively valuable in those colonies. (2603-4.) [*By the Committee.*] Did not the old colonies undertake the primary responsibility of their own defence, England contributing? now England undertakes the primary responsibility, and calls upon the colony to contribute.—I do not know whether that is quite a correct way of describing it. At that time the whole state of the world was so different to what it is now that you can hardly draw any comparison between the two. The colonies were not attacked upon their own ground by the great armies of civilised Powers; their principal danger was from Indian tribes, or from irregular forces of the French. (2605.) The French troops were very small indeed. [In 1763 the French in Canada numbered 60,000 or 70,000, the English colonies about

1,500,000. Massachusetts alone 240,000, and Massachusetts and Connecticut, the States nearest Canada, about 400,000.]

2617. The troops cost very little more (in garrisons at Kingston, Quebec and Halifax) than at home. (2620.) The Imperial Government must keep up a certain amount of regular army, and I think that a portion of that army is better quartered in those fortifications than at home.

2621. Do not garrisons being placed at those stations deter the colonists from providing the garrisons themselves?—I see no appearance of that. [See Lord Herbert's evidence, 3638.] Canada did make a considerable effort in raising and disciplining a militia. Nova Scotia and New Brunswick have declined to do so, from the simple reason that they apprehend no danger.

2622. [*By the Committee.*] In the war of 1812, although Canada raised a militia, she did not pay towards raising troops?—The danger to Canada during that war with the United States was entirely brought upon her by our most impolitic conduct towards the United States. (2623.) Canada justly felt that she was only suffering from her connection with us. (2624.) Where a war is created by our colonial relations, whether the colony ought to bear the expenses of the war, I would not lay down any abstract rules beforehand; when the case arises we must act according to the circumstances that exist.

2630. [*By Mr. Adderley.*] In the wars between Canada and the Indians, I find that the fresh reinforcements sent from Europe, in February, 1690, massacred the Indians, that they cut up the prisoners in pieces and made soup for their Indian allies who accompanied them. Does your Lordship anticipate that the Dutch or British settlers in any part of the world could be guilty of any atrocities such as these?—I cannot answer that. I do not think it applies in the least to the principle I have laid down.

2626. Since the time of Napoleon the efforts in war are directed to the main seat of government. In future wars, the whole struggle will be at home, or in the immediate vicinity.

2633. Out of the total of colonial receipts (from the Dutch colonies), £9,800,000, £5,300,000 came under the head of profit of sale of colonial produce. Hence the apparent tribute paid by Java to the mother country is not revenue, but profit derived from what is practically the great commercial monopoly in the hands of the Government. Holland probably loses far more by that monopoly than she gains by her apparent surplus. Spain also.

VII. *Extracts from the Evidence of* JOHN ROBERT GODLEY, *Under-Secretary of War.*

2069. The leading principle of my plan (rather it is the plan of Sir William Denison, an able and experienced colonial Governor), is colonial responsibility and management, and as a rule the contribution of the Imperial Government, if any, in the shape of money only. This was the system pursued by the old American colonies. (2086.) I have always said I would do what Lord Grey did in dealing with the Australian colonies [announcing to them his policy without consulting them. See evidence of Duke of Newcastle, 2946 ; Earl Grey, 2531-2 ; Merivale, 2496, 2521-2-4-5].

2070. Not one of the old colonies was ever conquered. [They were always the most populous communities of European origin in America. They were more populous in 1660 than the French in Canada in 1760, and in 1763 they numbered more than one million, but the French not more than sixty or seventy thousand. Nor have any other English colonies been conquered.] (2072.) The analogy between the old American colonies and those of the present day is complete as far as regards this question.

2093. I believe colonies add to our weakness. I have never seen a criticism upon the power and troops of England without observing that the writer considered the necessity of protecting colonies all over the world as the main element of our weakness. [A number of faithful allies—colonies—in all parts of the world adds greatly to our strength. Earl Grey's colonial policy.]

2115. The old colonies made war in the West Indies and other parts of America.

2177. Within the last twenty years we have been three or four times on the verge of a war with America upon purely colonial questions in which this country was not interested. [None of the colonies have involved England in war, but Canada has been involved in two wars on questions of Imperial policy now condemned by English statesmen. *See* Merivale's evidence, 2457; Lord Grey's evidence, 2622.]

2176, 2192. The colonies should be responsible primarily for their own defence, and England should contribute her quota on the ground that the colonies are involved in England's foreign policy,—her assistance being only in the shape of contribution—one half and one half would be a fair compromise, but I should be satisfied with any other ratio. (2193.) The assistance not to vary with the danger to which a particular colony is exposed!

2194. (*By the Committee.*) You think that the existence upon the frontier of Canada of a first-class

Power, with which Canada is liable to be involved in war, not by her own act, but by the policy of the Home Government, should be no element in calculating the assistance to be offered to Canada?—*My opinion is that it should not!*

2197. The French power in America, during the time of the old colonies, far exceeded that of the United States now, for aggressive purposes. [The population of the old colonies in 1660 was 80,000, while the French a century later were not 70,000. The English were upon the Atlantic, the French on the St. Lawrence, separated by hundreds of miles; vast forests, rivers, and hostile Indian tribes intervening.]

2198. Would advise the policy adopted by Earl Grey in 1851, towards the Australian colonies [announcing to the colonists the Imperial policy, but objecting to consult them—11th Resolution of Report], irrespective of the effect thereby produced upon the feelings and attachments of the colonists.

2063. The action of the Imperial troops in New Zealand lately has not been satisfactory to the colonists. (2164.) Mr. Fitzgerald, superintendent of Canterbury, and prime minister of the colony at the time, thus writes: 'Government formally declines our offer to volunteer to the Taranaki war. The Queen's army is hanging like an incubus on the colony, doing nothing itself and preventing any one else.' (2188.) I know that all the colonists are dissatisfied with the way the war has been carried on.

2691. We spend about £40,000 a year on the defence of the Bahamas; so that since the peace of 1814, we have spent nearly two millions of money in defending them, and during all that time we have never had a force there that could have resisted the crews of two frigates. (2094.) The circumstances of the West Indies are not such as to call for the necessity of our paying for their police, any more than for their roads or their civil officers.

VIII. *Extracts from the Evidence of* Mr. WALTER BRODIE, *Member of the New Zealand Legislature for four Years.*

2874. (*By Mr. Adderley.*) I understand you think that the control which the English Government retains over native affairs is the sole ground why England should pay for the troops in New Zealand?—Certainly. (2876.) New Zealand has now 4,000 or 5,000 militiamen or riflemen, under the command of two officers of the army. (2878.) These are a great deal better than the regular troops of the English army to deal with the natives,—they are much more willing to follow them into the woods than the military. This has been proved in the present war. (2872.) The Executive of New Zealand have no control over the affairs of the natives.

IX. *Extracts from the Evidence of* Mr. ELLIOT, *Assistant Under-Secretary of State for the Colonies, and connected with the Office for thirty Years.*

29. Lord Grey informed the Governor General of Canada in 1851, and subsequently the Duke of Newcastle and Sir George Grey in 1854, and Mr. Labouchere in 1856 did the same, that the time was come when they must expect a less amount of exertion on the part of this country to contribute towards their military defence. Troops would be reduced to the garrisons of Montreal and Quebec. (78.) This was addressed to Canada, but applied to all the North American colonies. The colonies cheerfully acquiesced—they showed their desire to assist this country and co-operate with her. [This was at the time of the Crimean war.]

74. Great Britain, with a view to national objects, keeps a large garrison at Halifax, one of the most important positions, in a strategical point of view, in North America. (86.) Similar to the garrisons in the Mediterranean and Bermuda. (75.) Quebec is also most important in a strategical point of view,

and is adequately garrisoned. (76.) We keep a large force at Halifax because it suits our own Imperial purposes. Nova Scotia does not want it.

138. There are 7,484 volunteers in Australia, including 1,500 in Tasmania. (345.) In British North America there are 10,006 volunteers:—4,456 in Canada, 2,350 in Nova Scotia, 1,800 in New Brunswick, 350 in Newfoundland, and 1,000 in Prince Edward's Island. [80,000 in Canada in 1865.]

X. *Extract from the Evidence of* Rear Admiral Erskine.

3204. Victoria pays £106 per man for sailors. In Tasmania it costs £127 per man; the colony pays nothing. (3257.) I think it necessary for Imperial interests that both Bermuda and Halifax should be maintained. (3286.) At Bermuda and in Australia I think it perfectly safe to substitute a naval force for troops, but not at Halifax.

XI. *Extracts from the Evidence of* The Right Hon. Robert Lowe, M.P., *and from* 1843–49 *Member of the Legislative Council of New South Wales.*

3330–1. I do not think it desirable to retain any troops in New South Wales. A government of that kind is not fit to be trusted with the disposition of Her Majesty's troops for any purpose whatever.

3335. When I lived at Sydney there was no income-tax, nor assessed taxes, nor excise, except on spirits, which probably was a benefit rather than a burden. Profits were large, wages very high. The mildness of the climate renders fuel almost unnecessary except for cooking, and enables people to do with little clothing. To tax the labourers of Leicestershire and Dorsetshire, to relieve such a community from a taxation required for its own defence, is a crying injustice. (3336.) Strange we should send people from England to defend the antipodes, while we leave the young men of Australia to grow up without the knowledge of arms.

3040. These being subject to our foreign policy, gives the colonies fair ground to ask for assistance in times of war.

3359. The Australians, were they trained, would make as fine soldiers as any in the world. There will be plenty to volunteer: no people better mounted: they make excellent sailors, and are full of spirit. Their particular industry is favourable for volunteering.

3405. Every soldier sent probably prevents a hundred colonists from taking up arms and drilling. [*Lord Herbert's ev.* 3638. *It is impossible to say upon what data Mr. Lowe founds his opinion. (3641.) A small force would be a nucleus around which the colonists would rally, and which would assist them in their military organization.*]

CHAPTER XI.

FUTURE OF THE COLONIES.

Colonies as Allies—Britain and Her Supremacy of the Seas—Rapid Growth of Navies of France, Russia, and United States—The Colonies as Maritime Powers—Their Strength added to that of England—Colonies and the Strength of the Empire—The Trent Affair—Attitude of Canada—Earl Derby on—What saved the Nation from War—Lord Dufferin on the Trent, and Canadian Loyalty—Can the great Branches of the Anglo-Saxon Family be consolidated into one Empire?—If not is it the fault of the Members or of the Head?—The Great Colonies—Old Colonies—Present Attitude of—Relation of Old Colonies to Parent State—Parliament and the Old Colonies—Virtually Independent and Loyal—Only Relations possible between England and those great Dependencies—Common Allegiance to the Throne—Legislatures of each—Independent to what Extent—Franchise in England: its Extension—Effects of—Universal Suffrage or greatly extended Franchise in England—In the Colonies—Great Majority of Voters in Colonies Owners of Farms—Reverse in England—Policy of the Empire—Who Dictates it—New Confederation of British America—Extent and Resources—Population—Area of Tillable Soil Compared with United States—Field for Surplus Population of England: its Position; Trade; Tonnage; third among Nations—Revenues — Surplus—Australia—Rapid Development—Present Position; Population; Trade; Revenue, &c.—

Independence of Colonies—Their Internal Policy—Relations to England—Ships; Colonies; and Commerce — Colonies the Foster-mothers of Commerce—Earl Grey and Earl Derby on Importance of Colonies to the Empire—Relations between Mother Country and Colonies. Pp. 196–208.

CAN the great branches of the Anglo-Saxon family be consolidated into one empire, or must they become independent and at the same time hostile nations? India, Ceylon, and Mauritius contain races little likely to amalgamate with the European, or to meet the melancholy fate to which the American and Australian aborigines seem doomed. The naval and military stations, the anti-slavery posts and smaller colonies, will doubtless remain as they are, dependent upon the power and will of the mother country.

But of the other great embryo States, what is to be their future? Of all the vast colonial empires of the nations of Europe, little now remains except to one, and that one lost in a foolish quarrel half a continent with thirteen vigorous and loyal States. Is there anything so unnatural and vicious in the relation of distant provinces to a central Power as to render continued union an impossibility? While weak, these tender offshoots cling to the parent stem; but must they necessarily fall off as soon as they attain strength sufficient to stand alone? If so, is it the fault of the system or of the members, and if of the members, of which? The one great example in English history throws the blame, in the opinion of English statesmen themselves, upon the parent State. The whole contest, through a long series of years, down to the breaking out of hostilities, gives us innumerable proofs of the loyalty and even affection of the colonists on the one hand, and of the haughty bearing, the injustice, the uncompromising spirit of the statesmen of the mother country on the other. Moderation would have prevented the rupture, and, when union should no longer be possible, would no doubt have secured the friendship of the younger members of the divided family. Enmity is perhaps a necessary consequence of the wrongs which embittered that violent separation. But are language, and blood, and religion, are a common history, a common civilization, common names, the soothing effects of a marvellous prosperity, and the lapse of time, even to generations, powerless to eradicate the feelings engendered in that quarrel? When youth attain to manhood, and leave the parental roof, around their distant and independent firesides, they and theirs still turn with a strong affection towards the old home. And why should not this be true of the sons and daughters of Britain in every clime? Or must all the great members of the Anglo-Saxon race, as they become independent communities, become also hostile to each other? United they might rule the world, and that rule would consist chiefly in preventing unjust wars. If this cannot be, and if the one great example already set must be followed by others, and Britain is never to have the alliance or even sympathy or moral support of any members of this great family of nations, at whose door will the fault lie? Such a prospect would be a dark one for the nation and the race. But the dark shades must be studied as well as the light, and those great events of a hundred years ago, leading to that melancholy revolt, cast their shadows far into the future, and darken every thought of the possibility of their repetition. If the British empire cannot be held together, is the error in the system, or in the extremities? or will it be, as it has been, the want of wisdom and moderation in the head?

If a number of steady allies, such allies as no independent States can be, add, while in their infancy, in the opinion of able English statesmen, so greatly to the moral influence and physical force of the empire, how much more will they do this in the future, when those now embryo States shall have attained a fuller development. The position of England as a great Power, her very commerce, and only to a less extent her manufactures, and her wealth, depend upon her supremacy of the seas. The rapid growth of the navies of two great European nations has imposed in a few short years immense burdens and incessant watchfulness upon the nation, for she must be always able and ready to cope with any two Powers on the ocean. Her naval expenditure has been doubled. Now there is added to these the unexampled development in the navy of a great maritime State on the other side of the Atlantic. No English statesman can contemplate with unconcern the amazing growth of the naval power of these great nations. The very position of this country as the champion of the seas, is a challenge and a humiliation to other great maritime nations. The prizes—power, empire, commerce, and wealth—are too great to allow the challenge to remain unaccepted, and so sure as time rolls on, a transatlantic Power, if not a European, will test the question of this maritime supremacy. Such are the elements that are being rapidly evolved for the solution of this problem so momentous to the future of England.

Under this new condition in the relations of Britain to other nations, the alliance of those great communities of loyal British subjects must be of increased importance to the continued stability and power of the empire. If need be, a dozen stalwart sons will come to the assistance of the mistress of the seas. They, like all Britain's offshoots, must be maritime States. One already in her mercantile marine is third amongst the great nations of the earth. Her fisheries on the coasts, in the Gulf of St. Lawrence, and on her inland waters, are the finest nursery for a navy which it would be possible to conceive. The existence of such powerful and devoted allies are sure not to be forgotten or their importance under-estimated by an enemy in contemplating the contingency of a war with Great Britain. In striking them an enemy does not strike any vulnerable part, nor in crushing them would he weaken the seat of power in the empire, but he would scatter his own force and waste his strength. It would be to these islands a mere tub tossed to the infuriated whale. While England would give home thrusts, the attacks upon those distant shores could decide nothing.

In contrast with the assertions of a narrow-minded class of writers, that the colonies bring weakness to England, and involve her in war—assertions at variance with every fact in her colonial history—we have the recorded opinions of many statesmen of the largest experience, that these dependencies add immensely to the moral influence of the nation, and even save her from war. The Trent affair is an example in point. No case could have occurred which would more forcibly illustrate this. An English mail steamer is boarded on the high seas, her passengers and mails seized and carried off by an American man-of-war. The aggressor is complimented by his government, and honoured and fêted by his countrymen, who declare, without a dissenting voice, that they will and must sustain the act. To the attitude assumed by the North American provinces, English statesmen attributed the preservation of peace. It will suffice here to quote Earl Derby in commenting on the speech from the throne in 1862, as expressing the opinions of the ablest English statesmen.

'While I give Her Majesty's Government the fullest credit for the firm and temperate manner in which they made their demand and sent out those reinforcements which were absolutely necessary to support the allegiance of our colonies, I rejoice to find that in the speech justice has been done to the spirit and unanimity with which all classes of Her Majesty's subjects in the North American provinces have come forward and shown their determination at all hazards—and the hazard of war would, in the first instance, have fallen on themselves—to maintain their allegiance [this they have always done—respected their oath in 1775, defended themselves in

1812-15, in 1837, etc.], and to support the honour and dignity of the British Crown. If there be one thing more than another that will tend to confirm the good understanding and peaceable relations that now exist between this country and the United States, it is the knowledge they must now have received of the utter delusion under which those persons within the States have laboured, that Canada and the North American provinces were eager for annexation with the States, and to sever their connection with Great Britain [what, in their whole history, could be referred to in proof of such assumptions?], and that, on the other hand, Great Britain would never venture upon a war with America, because she would always fear the willing annexation of Canada. That delusion is, I hope, now dissipated for ever, and its dissipation will form an important element in our future relations with America, and tend to secure us against the dangers of war with that country.' (*Hansard*, 1862.)

Lord Dufferin, in moving the address, in reply to the speech from the throne, on February 6, 1862, expresses, on the part of the Government, the following opinion:—

'No one can have failed to remark with extreme satisfaction the loyal and patriotic spirit which has been evoked in Canada by the prospect of an American war. Without a moment's hesitation, with an unanimity of sentiment which could not have been exceeded in this country, with the certainty of having to bear the brunt of a formidable attack along a comparatively unguarded frontier, the Canadian people manifested an amount of energy and determination which has well merited the affectionate admiration of the mother country. From henceforth the loyalty of Canada is as completely established as that of Middlesex or Kent.'

Even the 'poor Irish emigrants formed themselves into regiments for the defence of their Queen and for the protection of her empire.' (*Hansard*, 1862.)

The old British colonists in America considered themselves not as parts of the realm of Great Britain within the legislative power of Parliament, but as dependants of the British Crown, the King being their supreme and sovereign lord. They had no direct political connection with each other, their relations being those of independent States. They claimed that they carried with them and enjoyed the rights and privileges of British subjects and the benefit of the common law of England; and 'their legislatures,' says Story (*Com.* i. 110), 'exercised the authority to abrogate every part of the common law except that which united the colonies to the parent State by the general ties of allegiance and dependency, and every part of the statute law except those Acts of Parliament which expressly prescribed rules for the colonies.'

All these infant States established local governments for themselves, one branch of which consisted of representatives of the burgesses freely chosen, although no provision was made in the first charters for a legislature, except in that of Maryland.

At a very early period these American settlements, especially those under proprietary and charter governments, claimed that no Act of Parliament could bind them without their own consent. Massachusetts, as early as 1640, opposed any interference on the part of Parliament. In this spirit she disregarded and evaded the Navigation Act of 1651, and in 1679 declared, in an address to the Crown, that 'those acts were an invasion of the rights, liberties, and properties of the subjects of His Majesty in the colonies, they not being represented in Parliament.'

For nearly a century and a half those young communities lived almost as free from the control of Parliament as if they had been—which, in fact, they virtually were—independent States. They made war and peace, and entered into treaties with the French, Dutch, and Indians. Their loyalty was unquestioned. They regarded themselves as British subjects, having one common interest, and forming one empire with the people of these islands, owing a common allegiance to one and the same sovereign. The struggle between the Parliament and the Crown under the Stuarts necessarily secured their sympathy for the Commons; and while they looked upon Parliament as Dr. Franklin, in his evidence before the House of Commons in 1766, says, as the bulwark of their liberties, yet they were extremely jealous of any interference from it, denying its authority, and even refusing any favours from it, on the ground that such an act might be an acknowledgment of the right of Parliament over them.

Parliament, in 1766, a century and a half after the foundation of the first governments in those infant States, declared that ' the colonies and plantations in America are subordinate unto and dependent upon the Crown and Parliament of Great Britain; and the King, with the advice and consent of Parliament, hath full power and authority to make laws and statutes to bind the colonies and people of America in all cases whatsoever.'

The New England States, forced by superior power, finally acknowledged the authority of Parliament to regulate trade and commerce, but denied it in regard to taxation and their internal affairs; and in 1768, Massachusetts, the centre and leading State of New England, in a circular to the other colonies, admitted 'that His Majesty's High Court of Parliament is the supreme legislative power over the whole empire,' but claimed that, as British subjects, they could not be taxed without their own consent. (*Story*, i. 130.) The southern colonies maintained the same view. In the Pennsylvania charter an express reservation was made of the power of taxation, yet it was contended that Parliament had no right to exercise it. The Congress of Nine States, assembled at New York in 1765, admitted that 'Parliament was the supreme legislature of the whole empire, and as such had an undoubted jurisdiction over the whole colonies, *so far as is consistent with our essential interests*,' while they declared—and this was the object of the congress—'that no taxes ever have been, or can be, constitutionally imposed upon them but by their respective legislatures.' (*Id.* 131.) But after the passage of the Stamp Act, in 1765, the authority of Parliament began again to be disputed, and the Declaration of Independence ignores its very existence, and treats the acts of oppression there named as the acts of the King, in combination 'with others,' for the overthrow of their liberties.

From their origin to their revolution the old American colonies manifested in all their history a sincere attachment to the throne. Only in their contest with Parliament could their loyalty be called in question, and this chiefly during the twenty years preceding 1775. In that struggle they considered that their rights and liberties were invaded. Parliament succeeded for a time in wringing from them the acknowledgment of its authority, but at the sacrifice of their allegiance. Communities virtually independent, and having their own legislatures, could not see the justice of yielding obedience to the enactments of a Parliament in whose councils they were not represented.

The history of all the great British colonies of the present day teaches the same lesson—discontent—and sometimes rebellion, growing out of the interference of Parliament. The clergy-reserves and rectories of Canada, the tariffs of all the North American provinces, the convict question of Australia, and the control of the aborigines of South Africa and New Zealand, are all instances in which the meddling of the Colonial Office and the assumptions of Parliament, have worked nothing but mischief. Why then should this policy be pursued? Those great and thriving communities of English origin, having their own legislatures, if worthy of self-government, cannot submit to the assumption of authority on the part of a legislature in which they are not represented. And if that power is never to be exercised, as it cannot be over any of those great communities, why is it retained? Is it as an emblem of power, and a badge of submission? In theory Parliament is omnipotent over the whole empire; in theory, then, a colonial government, however complete, can be no more than municipal.

There would remain as the basis of union between the parent State and those great countries abroad, a common allegiance to the throne—the fountain of honour and the emblem of power. Each would have its own legislature independent of all others within its own boundary. The questions of peace and war would necessarily rest with the British cabinet, giving due attention to the opinions as expressed by their ministry, of those members of the empire more especially affected by the policy of the central authority. Some of those colonies will speedily rise to great power. Their populations are sensitive to an extreme on every question affecting their independence. Any remaining bond of union with the throne or the Parliament which would remind them that they were not in every respect on an equality with their fellow-subjects of these islands could but weaken the connection. An empire so varied, so extended, and composed of parts having such diverse interests, will have naturally too many elements of dissolution without creating artificial ones. If the Crown is to hold all in allegiance, the crown must be to all the same. The relation must be of the simplest nature. The danger will arise from the interference of Parliament and its ministers in matters beyond their proper jurisdiction, and they must relax their hold of the distant members, that the crown may increase it.

Complaint is even now made by the great organs of public opinion,* that the policy of the empire is controlled, not by those who bear the burdens of state, but by those whose circumstances exempt them from taxation, while their numbers make them all-powerful at the polls. The first step was taken in 1832 towards a greatly extended franchise— towards, in effect, universal suffrage; for to this the movement inevitably tends. The anomalies which exist in the English representative system are no doubt in part susceptible of adjustment without shifting the basis of it. But a measure limited to the more equal representation of numbers, in the various constituencies of the United Kingdom, would not satisfy the advocates for the extension of the franchise. Universal suffrage, or even the lowering of the money qualification of the voter, would be a very different thing in England with 50 per cent. of the population civic, and in the British provinces with only 20 to 30 per cent. civic, and 70

* *Times*, August 12, 1864.

P

to 80 agricultural; and this agricultural population owners of the land they cultivate, and accustomed in their municipalities to representative institutions. Such agricultural population is, too, a highly conservative population, well educated, and owners of farms of 100 to 200 acres. In England the majority of the voters would be made up of one interest—the trading, manufacturing, and commercial. Nor is the most dangerous feature in a low franchise or universal suffrage, that every man may vote; but that in such a state those having the lowest qualification, and especially the ignorant and violent, are sure to be at the polls, and this very circumstance keeps away the men of retiring habits. The elected become more and more the representatives of violence and ignorance.

The lowering the money qualification from £10 to £6 would reach not more than 240,000 out of the 4,000,000 of the unrepresented, and those by no means the most intelligent. A large class amongst professional men—clerks, writers, &c.—would still be left out. To give universal suffrage—to which all arguments founded upon an *à priori* right tend, and the favourite argument of the advocates for the extension of the franchise—would be to add 4,000,000 of voters, mostly from one class. This would virtually disfranchise the 1,000,000, the most intelligent and wealthy—the tax-payers—to whom the right is now restricted. In contradistinction to this unreasoning cry for manhood and even womanhood* suffrage, the delegates from all the provinces, in their councils on the confederation of British America, were unanimous in their opinion that the franchise should be raised instead of lowered; and this in countries where 70 per cent. of the population are owners of the estates on which they vote.

If complaint is now made of the too great influence of one class of voters,† the grounds of such complaints must be stronger in the future. This class will dictate the policy of the empire—the policy, too, towards the colonies, and over British subjects even better qualified than the dictators to take part in representative government. Parliament is said to be the most renowned of debating clubs, and every minister knows the difficulty of keeping within due bounds the abundant liberty of speech on all questions of foreign and colonial policy. The unjust strictures, the careless yet ungenerous allusions to colonial affairs, embitter the relations. The colonists, youthful as they are represented to be, show more prudence in their dis-

---

* Address of J. S. Mill to Electors of Westminster, April 1865.
† *Times*, August 12, 1864.

cussions, as every unfavourable allusion to Parliament is by common consent a forbidden topic, unless, indeed, when called forth in reply to what has already been said by Lords or Commons.

The debates in Parliament in 1763 did more than all other agencies or causes combined to embitter the minds of the Americans, not even excepting the odious stamp and tea taxes. 'We are cowards, are we?' was the retort of the militia at Bunker's Hill, as they pressed upon the British troops. This reproach—some thoughtless expression in Parliament—against the colonists was remembered in the heat of battle even more vividly than the acts of oppression which had caused them to rebel.

The new confederation of British provinces in North America—Canada and the maritime colonies—embraces chiefly the valley of the St. Lawrence and Great Lakes, and covers an area of 450,000 square miles—as large as France, Spain, and Portugal, or eight times the area of England. It lies in the most favoured part of the temperate zone, from latitude 42° to the Laurentine chain of mountains, which divide the waters flowing into the St. Lawrence from those falling into Hudson's Bay. This is now its assumed limits. But Canada, as ceded to Great Britain in 1763, extends from the parallel of 42° to the Arctic ocean, and from the Atlantic to the Pacific, embracing more than half of the American continent; so that the new government, should the North-West and the Pacific provinces fall into the scheme, would rule over a country of more than 4,000,000 of square miles, and larger by one million than the American Republic, and possessing probably as much arable land; for the vast desert in that republic from the Mississippi to near the Pacific may be set off against the frozen regions in British America. Neither on nor around the arid American desert is there any compensation for the barren waste, while the waters that wash the inhospitable regions of the Northern confederation swarm with the most prolific fisheries, from the banks of Newfoundland and the shores of Labrador through the innumerable islands, bays, and inlets of the three great oceans that encircle British America, to Vancouver's, the queen of the Pacific. As high as latitude 60° in the interior 'wheat is grown with profit,' and where wheat will grow we have a climate most propitious to the cereals, grasses, and root crops, and most favourable for the ox, the sheep, and the horse. South of latitude 60° there is an area equal to all Europe, and on the very northern border of this immense territory 'wheat grows with profit.' That there is much that is inhospitable in the north and east is a necessity; these facts are referred to here merely to show the great extent of arable land throughout British America, offering a most inviting field for the surplus population of the old world. The St. Lawrence, with its gulf and great lakes, the seat of this newly consolidated nation, is in importance equal to the Baltic, and waters even a greater and more fertile country. The largest ocean steamers ascend to Quebec, 500 miles from the Atlantic; and those drawing twenty-two feet of water, to Montreal. The St. Lawrence canals, with a lockage of 230 feet, admit vessels of 600 tons to Lake Ontario, a thousand miles from the ocean; and the Welland canal (300 feet lockage and thirty miles long) passes vessels of 400 tons to the Upper Lakes. This gives 2000 miles of inland navigation, with only some fifty miles of canal, to the head of Lake Superior, and is the direct highway to the vast and fertile plains of Lake Winnipeg and the Saskatchewan.

The new confederation would be formed under the most auspicious circumstances. The existence of its several members has been little more than an embryo existence. To-day it is a nation of four millions of people, of boundless territory, of vast and varied resources, with a climate the most salubrious and invigorating, and the most propitious to all the valuable products of the temperate zone, which here yield the husbandman a better return than in any other portion of the American continent.* It possesses a trade and mercantile marine the fourth, if not the third, amongst the nations of the earth; 2000 miles of magnificent inland navigation on the St. Lawrence and lakes, exclusive of its other great rivers and smaller lakes, and 2500 miles of railway; 700,000 men between twenty and sixty years of age, or half a million of able-bodied men from eighteen to forty-five, and 70,000 sailors; and a population accustomed to those hardy pursuits peculiar to a country of vast forests abounding in game, and of great rivers and lakes swarming with fish.

The trade—imports and exports—of the confederated provinces amounted in 1864 to nearly thirty millions sterling; with five million tons of shipping on the sea, and seven millions on the inland lakes in the Canadian trade alone. The revenue for the same year was $14,223,000 (nearly £3,000,000), and the expenditure $13,350,000; leaving nearly one million dollars surplus. The products of the soil in 1860 were estimated at $150,000,000 in value, and the cultivated lands at $1,500,000,000.

At the antipodes we find a most marvellous development in the population and resources of those vigorous British communities which are spreading themselves over that continent island. The first

* See the last two decennial census of Canada (1852 & 1861).

permanent British settlement in Australia was composed of 850 convicts with their military guard, the governor and his staff—about 1,100 persons in all. These landed at Botany Bay in January 1788, four years after the settlement of Upper Canada. At the end of three-quarters of a century from this unpromising beginning we have in Australia, including Tasmania and New Zealand, seven colonies, with a population in (1864) of little less than one and a half millions, in an area of 2,500,000 square miles; a trade of £50,000,000; a revenue of some £7,000,000; 30,000,000 of sheep, supplying to British looms 100,000,000lbs. wool annually of an export value of £5,000,000; 4,000,000 of horned cattle; and half a million of horses. These great results have been achieved chiefly during the last twelve or fifteen years.

The complete independence of these great communities of Anglo-Saxons can be only a question of time. Both possess vast areas of the most fertile soil and boundless mineral wealth. Their rapid development in material prosperity, their free institutions, their admirable school and municipal organizations, the energy of the populations, and the wisdom and moderation shown in moulding their political fabrics, are the best promise of the future. We have no example in history of better-governed states. Some of them were at first encumbered with the feudal system, and other establishments of a past age and a widely different civilization; these they have quietly rid themselves of, without endangering the peace or well-being of society.

The thirteen original colonies at the time of their revolt, a few years previous to the settlement of Australia, Canada West, and New Brunswick, had a population of 2,600,000. At the last census, in 1860, they were 30,000,000. After a century and a half from their foundation, these old colonies embraced a population of not more than two and a half millions. Upper Canada and Australia, eighty years after their settlement, have each a million and a half. In population and wealth, Canada, during the last quarter of a century, has shown a more rapid increase than the republic on her border. From the past, then, we are justified in the inference that these now great and flourishing British provinces will speedily become populous and powerful nations. Of their conquest and subjection to any foreign power there would seem to be little probability. How long they may remain a part of the empire that planted them will depend upon the wisdom of the rulers of both. An equality in rights and duties would seem the only basis for a continued union. Each must be willing to bear the burdens common to all. The throne might then long continue the seat of empire, the emblem of power and the fountain of honour, equally to every member of this great family of nations.

Great maritime powers in all ages have had colonial possessions, larger or smaller. This is, in the first instance, one legitimate result of commerce; but after being established, colonies, as we have shown, foster that commerce more than other countries.

Ships, colonies, and commerce' express high interests of a maritime state. If commerce called into existence the shipping, colonies may now be said to be the chief foster-mother of both, and we might almost reduce the motto to the one word 'colonies.' The chief influence, the honour, and wealth from these fall to the parent state, although most English statesmen are slow to acknowledge it. These, too, lessen instead of increase the naval expenditure, the chief of which, on colonial account, is for the naval and military stations at Malta, Gibraltar, Bermuda, and in the East and West Indies; but none or little where the great dependencies of the crown are. Give these up, and naval stations must take their place.

Earl Grey and Earl Derby have spoken with a frankness and generosity on the important services rendered to the mother country by the colonies, rare amongst English statesmen.

'The British colonial empire ought to be maintained, principally because I do not consider that the nation would be justified in throwing off the responsibility it has incurred by the acquisition of this dominion, and because I believe that *much of the power and influence of this country depend upon its having large colonial possessions in different parts of the world. The possession of a number of steady allies in all quarters of the globe adds greatly to the strength of any nation,* while no alliance between independent states can be so close and intimate as the connection which unites the colonies to the United Kingdom as parts of the great British Empire.

'Nor ought it to be forgotten that the power of a nation does not depend merely on the amount of physical force it can command, but rests in no small degree upon opinion and moral influence; in this respect British power would be diminished by the loss of the colonies to a degree which it would be difficult to estimate. The tie which binds together all the distant and different portions of the British Empire, so that their united strength may be wielded for the common protection, must be regarded as an object of extreme importance to the interests of the mother country and her dependencies.' (Letter 1, p. 12.)

Earl Derby, in referring to the settlement of the Trent affair at the opening of Parliament in 1862, spoke specially of the spirit and unanimity with which all classes of Her Majesty's subjects in the North American provinces had come forward and shown their determination—exposed as they were to invasion, and sure to have their country made the battle-field—to maintain their allegiance, and to support the honour and dignity of the British crown. He declared that if there be any one thing that would tend to confirm the good understanding and peaceable relations between this country and the United States, it was the knowledge they must now have received of the utter delusion under which those persons within the States have laboured, that Canada and the North American provinces were eager for annexation with the States, and that Great Britain would never venture upon a war with America, because she would fear the willing annexation of Canada. That delusion was, he hoped, dissipated for ever, and its dissipation would form an important element in our relations with America, and tend to secure us against the dangers of war.—(*Hansard*, 1862.)

Carthage, for seven centuries, held along the shores and over the islands of the Mediterranean three hundred cities tributary as the fruit of her maritime supremacy, and Rome, for five centuries, kept in subjection half the then known world. Why should the influence of the British throne be less over communities of similar origin, religion, and laws than was Carthage with her navy, and Rome with her army, over the discordant elements which made up their empires? In no Carthaginian or Roman sense of citizenship would we advocate the subjection of any member of the empire to the throne. But, with two thousand years' experience over those renowned states from which to draw lessons of wisdom, is it impossible to find a basis of union receiving the cordial consent of every member of this great family of nations, as enduring a foundation of empire as the flag of Carthage or the spear of Rome?

The old English colonies in America claimed to be absolutely free from the control of Parliament, and only submitted finally to superior power, and to an assumption that caused the revolution. Why should not every member of this great family of nations stand in the same relation to the throne, which these islands now sustain, and which the old colonies claimed? Each would have its own independent Legislature, absolute within its own dominions, but owing allegiance to the same sovereign. The questions of peace and war would still rest with the throne, by and with the advice, as now, of the Imperial ministry, allowing some just influence to those other great commonwealths affected by such decisions, or which in case of war should contribute their reasonable share. Such union would be the best guarantee for peace within her own widely-extended dominions, and the strongest protection against insult or assault from without. The high objects and interests common to all are surely motives strong enough to cement such union. At all events it would be wiser for the nation to fix its attention upon some definite object to be attained in the relations of the different members of the empire, than to leave all to chance or to circumstances. Commerce—the controlling genius, if not the Divinity of the nation—is now the guiding star in our foreign relations, and commerce is blind to everything but its own interest; it knows no law but profit. Why then should not the statesmen of the mother country and of the colonies seek some sounder principles of union, equitable to all, and promising a closer and more enduring connection? Why need it be a necessity that the moment a province attains independence or sufficient strength to stand alone, that epoch in its history should also be the epoch of its entire separation from the empire? In such a union as here contemplated Britain would be the chief gainer. Here would rest the executive authority, the greatest concentration of wealth, and the centre of her now vast and daily expanding commerce.

By some these aspirations may be looked upon as

the offspring of the imagination only. But they are not mere sentiments, barren of good. The advancement of man in all that is connected with high civilization and the amelioration of his condition upon the earth, is sought for chiefly in the histories of the great empires of ancient and modern times. Even the Greeks, although broken up during a part of their history into small commonwealths, were a numerous and powerful people, and for a time the ruling race.

If it be a sentiment to wish to retain under one government the two hundred and thirty millions that make up the British Empire, it is a noble sentiment. The rulers, who would be chiefly those of our own race in every part of those vast dominions, would meet with many and great occasions to call into play the highest qualities of the statesman. Then none will deny the good influence of such a connection upon the numerous and diverse races in every quarter of the globe that are brought into intimate union with a great Christian nation; with a people who, more than any others, have learned to unite good government with ample liberty.

Many questions will, no doubt, arise to disturb the relations between the parent State and the distant members of the empire. Some of these have been referred to in the preceding chapters, and they may be expected to reappear in our future history under new modifications.

The disputes growing out of the rights claimed by parliament, and resisted by the old colonies, ended in the American revolution of 1775. Again and again, since that period, attempts have been made to enforce the same abstract theory, the omnipotence of parliament, over every part of the empire. This right has been assumed, even in local matters, since the granting of parliamentary governments to the colonies.

The foreign policy of the whole empire now conducted by the crown and parliament, can scarcely remain unquestioned under all circumstances when those now young commonwealths shall have become populous and powerful states. Involved in this is the question of defence, for while the Imperial government may draw the colonies into war against their will and against their interests, she must hold herself responsible for the results of her diplomacy.

But the manufacturing and commercial interests, the most powerful and active interests in England, have the chief influence in the home and foreign policy of the nation; and these are the classes which have least sympathy with our colonial empire.

The questions of the customs and revenue, the fine lines drawn between protective and revenue tariffs, must bring, as they have brought, the policy of the new and the old societies into conflict. A country overburdened with population, having a vast accumulated wealth, and seeking not to establish manufactories and other industries, but to find markets for her products, can but imperfectly understand the condition of those communities whose wants are the reverse of these. England, agricultural, would have a population of scarcely 5,000,000; manufacturing and commercial England has 20,000,000. New England, too, with her rocky and barren soil, is the most wealthy and populous part of the Republic. High tariffs have attracted capital and labour; manufactures and commerce have followed. These again create further demand for labour. During the last seven years more than three millions of immigrants have landed at New York alone. Such additional populations react favourably upon the agricultural, create local markets, and help to bear the burdens of state.

Those young countries, with their vast territories of the richest soil, now unoccupied, seeking labour and capital to utilize the undeveloped resources of their mines and fisheries, their forests and fields, cannot remain uninfluenced by such examples of prosperity in states possessing so many points of resemblance to their own.

APPENDICES.

Appendices

APPENDIX A.

Resolutions adopted at a Conference of Delegates from the Provinces of Canada, Nova Scotia, and New Brunswick, and the Colonies of Newfoundland and Prince Edward Island, held at the City of Quebec, 10th October 1864, as the Basis of a proposed Confederation of those Provinces and Colonies.

1. The best interests and present and future prosperity of British North America will be promoted by a federal union under the Crown of Great Britain, provided such union can be effected on principles just to the several provinces.

2. In the federation of the British North American Provinces the system of government best adapted under existing circumstances to protect the diversified interests of the several provinces and secure efficiency, harmony, and permanency in the working of the union—would be a general government charged with matters of common interest to the whole country, and local governments for each of the Canadas and for the provinces of Nova Scotia, New Brunswick, and Prince Edward Island, charged with the control of local matters in their respective sections—provision being made for the admission into the union on

equitable terms of Newfoundland, the North-West Territory, British Columbia, and Vancouver.

3. In framing a constitution for the general government, the Conference, with a view to the perpetuation of our connection with the mother country, and to the promotion of the best interests of the people of these provinces, desire to follow the model of the British constitution, so far as our circumstances will permit.

4. The executive authority or government shall be vested in the sovereign of the United Kingdom of Great Britain and Ireland, and be administered according to the well-understood principles of the British constitution by the sovereign personally, or by the representative of the sovereign duly authorized.

5. The sovereign or representative of the sovereign shall be a commander-in-chief of the land and naval militia forces.

6. There shall be a general legislature or parliament for the federated provinces, composed of a Legislative Council and a House of Commons.

7. For the purpose of forming the Legislative Council, the federated provinces shall be considered as consisting of three divisions—1st, Upper Canada; 2nd, Lower Canada; 3rd, Nova Scotia, New Brunswick, and Prince Edward Island,—each division with an equal representation in the Legislative Council.

8. Upper Canada shall be represented in the Legislative Council by twenty-four members, Lower Canada by twenty-four members, and the three maritime provinces by twenty-four members, of which Nova Scotia shall have ten, New Brunswick, ten, and Prince Edward Island four members.

9. The colony of Newfoundland shall be entitled to

enter the proposed union, with a representation in the Legislative Council of four members.

10. The North-West Territory, British Columbia, and Vancouver shall be admitted into the union, on such terms and conditions as the parliament of the federated provinces shall deem equitable, and as shall receive the assent of Her Majesty; and in the case of the province of British Columbia or Vancouver, as shall be agreed to by the legislature of such province.

11. The members of the Legislative Council shall be appointed by the Crown under the great seal of the general government, and shall hold office during life: if any legislative councillor shall, for two consecutive sessions of parliament, fail to give his attendance in the said council, his seat shall thereby become vacant.

12. The members of the Legislative Council shall be British subjects by birth or naturalization, of the full age of thirty years, shall possess a continuous real property qualification of four thousand dollars over and above all encumbrances, and shall be and continue worth that sum over and above their debts and liabilities, but in the case of Newfoundland and Prince Edward Island, the property may be either real or personal.

13. If any question shall arise as to the qualification of a legislative councillor, the same shall be determined by the council.

14. The first selection of the members of the Legislative Council shall be made, except as regards Prince Edward Island, from the legislative councils of the various provinces, so far as a sufficient number be found qualified and willing to serve; such members shall be appointed by the Crown at the recommendation of the general executive

government, upon the nomination of the respective local governments, and in such nomination due regard shall be had to the claims of the members of the Legislative Council of the Opposition in each province, so that all political parties may as nearly as possible be fairly represented.

15. The Speaker of the Legislative Council (unless otherwise provided by parliament) shall be appointed by the Crown from among the members of the Legislative Council, and shall hold office during pleasure, and shall only be entitled to a casting vote on an equality of votes.

16. Each of the twenty-four legislative councillors representing Lower Canada in the Legislative Council of the general legislature, shall be appointed to represent one of the twenty-four electoral divisions mentioned in Schedule A of chapter first of the Consolidated Statutes of Canada, and such councillor shall reside or possess his qualification in the division he is appointed to represent.

17. The basis of representation in the House of Commons shall be population, as determined by the official census every ten years: and the number of members at first shall be 194, distributed as follows:—

Upper Canada	82
Lower Canada	65
Nova Scotia	19
New Brunswick	15
Newfoundland	8
and Prince Edward Island	5

18. Until the official census of 1871 has been made up, there shall be no change in the number of representatives from the several sections.

19. Immediately after the completion of the census of

1871, and immediately after every decennial census thereafter, the representation from each section in the House of Commons shall be re-adjusted on the basis of population.

20. For the purpose of such re-adjustments, Lower Canada shall always be assigned sixty-five members, and each of the other sections shall at each re-adjustment receive, for the ten years then next succeeding, the number of members to which it will be entitled on the same ratio of representation to population as Lower Canada will enjoy according to the census last taken by having sixty-five members.

21. No reduction shall be made in the number of members returned by any section, unless its population shall have decreased relatively to the population of the whole union, to the extent of five per centum.

22. In computing at each decennial period the number of members to which each section is entitled, no fractional parts shall be considered, unless when exceeding one half the number entitling to a member, in which case a member shall be given for each such fractional part.

23. The legislature of each province shall divide such province into the proper number of constituencies, and define the boundaries of each of them.

24. The local legislature of each province may, from time to time, alter the electoral districts for the purposes of representation in such local legislature, and distribute the representatives to which the province is entitled, in any manner such legislature may think fit.

25. The number of members may at any time be increased by the general parliament, regard being had to the proportionate rights then existing.

26. Until provisions are made by the general parliament,

all the laws which, at the date of the proclamation constituting the union, are in force in the provinces respectively, relating to the qualification and disqualification of any person to be elected or to sit or vote as a member of the Assembly in the said provinces respectively—and relating to the qualification or disqualification of voters, and to the oaths to be taken by voters, and to returning officers and their powers and duties—and relating to the proceedings at elections—and to the period during which such elections may be continued, and relating to the trial of controverted elections, and the proceedings incident thereto, and relating to the vacating of seats of members and to the issuing and execution of new writs in case of any seat being vacated otherwise than by a dissolution,—shall respectively apply to elections of members to serve in the House of Commons, for places situate in those provinces respectively.

27. Every House of Commons shall continue for five years from the day of the return of the writs choosing the same, and no longer, subject, nevertheless, to be sooner prorogued or dissolved by the governor.

28. There shall be a session of the general parliament once at least in every year, so that a period of twelve calendar months shall not intervene between the last sitting of the general parliament in one session and the first sitting thereof in the next session.

29. The general parliament shall have power to make laws for the peace, welfare, and good government of the federated provinces (saving the sovereignty of England), and especially laws respecting the following subjects:—

    1. The public debt and property.
    2. The regulation of trade and commerce.

3. The imposition or regulation of duties of customs on imports and exports, except on exports of timber, logs, masts, spars, deals, and sawn lumber, and of coal and other minerals.
4. The imposition or regulation of excise duties.
5. The raising of money by all or any other modes or systems of taxation.
6. The borrowing of money on the public credit.
7. Postal service.
8. Lines of steam or other ships, railways, canals, and other works, connecting any two or more of the provinces together or extending beyond the limits of any province.
9. Lines of steamships between the federated provinces and other countries.
10. Telegraphic communication and the incorporation of telegraph companies.
11. All such works as shall, although lying wholly within any province, be specially declared by the Acts authorising them to be for the general advantage.
12. The census.
13. Militia—military and naval service and defence.
14. Beacons, buoys, and lighthouses.
15. Navigation and shipping.
16. Quarantine.
17. Sea coast and inland fisheries.
18. Ferries between any province and a foreign country, or between any two provinces.
19. Currency and coinage.
20. Banking, incorporation of banks, and the issue of paper money.

21. Savings banks.
22. Weights and measures.
23. Bills of exchange and promissory notes.
24. Interest.
25. Legal tender.
26. Bankruptcy and insolvency.
27. Patents of invention and discovery.
28. Copyrights.
29. Indians and lands reserved for the Indians.
30. Naturalization and aliens.
31. Marriage and divorce.
32. The criminal law, excepting the constitution of Courts of Criminal Jurisdiction, but including procedure in criminal matters.
33. Rendering uniform all or any of the laws relative to property and civil rights in Upper Canada, Nova Scotia, New Brunswick, Newfoundland, and Prince Edward Island, and rendering uniform the procedure of all or any of the courts in these provinces; but any statute for this purpose shall have no force or authority in any province until sanctioned by the legislature thereof.
34. The establishment of a General Court of Appeal for the federated provinces.
35. Immigration.
36. Agriculture.
37. And generally respecting all matters of a general character, not specially and exclusively reserved for the local governments and legislatures.

30. The general government and parliament shall have all powers necessary or proper for performing the obligations of the federated provinces, as part of the British empire, to foreign countries, arising under treaties between Great Britain and such countries.

31. The general parliament may also, from time to time, establish additional courts, and the general government may appoint judges and officers thereof, when the same shall appear necessary or for the public advantage, in order to the due execution of the laws of parliament.

32. All courts, judges, and officers of the several provinces shall aid, assist, and obey the general government in the exercise of its rights and powers, and for such purposes shall be held to be courts, judges, and officers of the general government.

33. The general government shall appoint and pay the judges of the superior courts in each province, and of the county courts of Upper Canada, and parliament shall fix their salaries.

34. Until the consolidation of the laws of Upper Canada, New Brunswick, Nova Scotia, Newfoundland, and Prince Edward Island, the judges of these provinces appointed by the general government shall be selected from their respective bars.

35. The judges of the courts of Lower Canada shall be selected from the bar of Lower Canada.

36. The judges of the Court of Admiralty now receiving salaries shall be paid by the general government.

37. The judges of the superior courts shall hold their offices during good behaviour, and shall be removable only on the address of both houses of parliament.

Local Government.

38. For each of the provinces there shall be an executive officer, styled the Lieutenant Governor, who shall be appointed by the Governor General in council, under the great seal of the federated provinces, during pleasure: such pleasure not to be exercised before the expiration of the first five years, except for cause: such cause to be communicated in writing to the Lieutenant Governor immediately after the exercise of the pleasure as aforesaid, and also by message to both houses of parliament, within the first week of the first session afterwards.

39. The Lieutenant Governor of each province shall be paid by the general government.

40. In undertaking to pay the salaries of the lieutenant governors, the Conference does not desire to prejudice the claim of Prince Edward Island upon the Imperial government for the amount now paid for the salary of the Lieutenant Governor thereof.

41. The local government and legislature of each province shall be constructed in such manner as the existing legislature of such province shall provide.

42. The local legislatures shall have power to alter or amend their constitution from time to time.

43. The local legislatures shall have power to make laws respecting the following subjects:—

1. Direct taxation and the imposition of duties on the export of timber, logs, masts, spars, deals, and sawn lumber, and of coals and other minerals.
2. Borrowing money on the credit of the province.
3. The establishment and tenure of local offices, and the appointment and payment of local officers.

4. Agriculture.
5. Immigration.
6. Education; saving the rights and privileges which the Protestant or Catholic minority in both Canadas may possess as to their denominational schools, at the time when the union goes into operation.
7. The sale and management of public lands, excepting lands belonging to the general government.
8. Sea coast and inland fisheries.
9. The establishment, maintenance, and management of penitentiaries, and of public and reformatory prisons.
10. The establishment, maintenance, and management of hospitals, asylums, charities, and eleemosynary institutions.
11. Municipal institutions.
12. Shop, saloon, tavern, auctioneer, and other licences.
13. Local works.
14. The incorporation of private or local companies, except such as relate to matters assigned to the general parliament.
15. Property and civil rights, excepting those portions thereof assigned to the general parliament.
16. Inflicting punishment by fine, penalties, imprisonment, or otherwise, for the breach of laws passed in relation to any subject within their jurisdiction.
17. The administration of justice, including the constitution, maintenance, and organization of the courts—both of civil and criminal jurisdiction, and including also the procedure in civil matters.
18. And generally all matters of a private or local nature, not assigned to the general parliament.

44. The power of respiting, reprieving, and pardoning prisoners convicted of crimes, and of commuting and remitting of sentences in whole or in part, which belongs of right to the Crown, shall be administered by the Lieutenant Governor of each province in council, subject to any instructions he may from time to time receive from the general government, and subject to any provisions that may be made in this behalf by the general parliament. [The Secretary of State for the Colonies wishes this power to rest in the Governor General.]

Miscellaneous.

45. In regard to all subjects over which jurisdiction belongs to both the general and local legislatures, the laws of the general parliament shall control and supersede those made by the local legislature, and the latter shall be void so far as they are repugnant to or inconsistent with the former.

46. Both the English and French languages may be employed in the general parliament and in its proceedings, and in the local legislature of Lower Canada, and also in the federal courts and in the courts of Lower Canada.

47. No lands or property belonging to the general or local government shall be liable to taxation.

48. All bills for appropriating any part of the public revenue, or for imposing any new tax or impost, shall originate in the House of Commons or the House of Assembly, as the case may be.

49. The House of Commons or House of Assembly shall not originate or pass any vote, resolution, address, or bill for the appropriation of any part of the public revenue, or of any tax or impost to any purpose, not first recom-

mended by message of the Governor General, or the Lieutenant Governor, as the case may be, during the session in which such vote, resolution, address, or bill is passed.

50. Any bill of the general parliament may be reserved in the usual manner for Her Majesty's assent, and any bill of the local legislatures may in like manner be reserved for the consideration of the Governor General.

51. Any bill passed by the general parliament shall be subject to disallowance by Her Majesty within two years, as in the case of bills passed by the legislatures of the said provinces hitherto; and in like manner any bill passed by a local legislature shall be subject to disallowance by the Governor General within one year after the passing thereof.

52. The seat of government of the federated provinces shall be Ottawa, subject to the Royal prerogative.

53. Subject to any future action of the respective local governments, the seat of the local government in Upper Canada shall be Toronto; of Lower Canada, Quebec; and the seats of the local governments in the other provinces shall be as at present.

Property and Liabilities.

54. All stocks, cash, bankers' balances, and securities for money belonging to each province, at the time of the union, except as hereinafter mentioned, shall belong to the general government.

55. The following public works and property of each province shall belong to the general government—to wit:—

    1. Canals;
    2. Public harbours;
    3. Lighthouses and piers;
    4. Steamboats, dredges, and public vessels;

>   5. River and lake improvements;
>   6. Railway and railway stocks, mortgages, and other debts due by railway companies;
>   7. Military roads;
>   8. Custom-houses, post-offices, and other public buildings, except such as may be set aside by the general government for the use of the local legislatures and governments;
>   9. Property transferred by the Imperial government and known as ordnance property;
>   10. Armories, drill sheds, military clothing, and munitions of war; and
>   11. Lands set apart for public purposes.

56. All lands, mines, minerals, and royalties vested in Her Majesty in the provinces of Upper Canada, Lower Canada, Nova Scotia, New Brunswick, and Prince Edward Island, for the use of such provinces, shall belong to the local government of the territory in which the same are so situate; subject to any trusts that may exist in respect to any of such lands or to any interest of other persons in respect of the same.

57. All sums due from purchasers or lessees of such lands, mines, or minerals at the time of the union, shall also belong to the local governments.

58. All assets connected with such portions of the public debt of any province as are assumed by the local governments, shall also belong to those governments respectively.

59. The several provinces shall retain all other public property therein, subject to the right of the general government to assume any lands or public property required for fortifications or the defence of the country.

60. The general government shall assume all the debts and liabilities of each province.

    61. The debt of Canada not specially assumed by Upper and Lower Canada respectively, shall not exceed at the time of the union . . $62,500,000

Nova Scotia shall enter the union with a debt not exceeding . . 8,000,000

And New Brunswick, with a debt not exceeding 7,000,000

    62. In case Nova Scotia or New Brunswick do not incur liabilities beyond those for which their governments are now bound, and which shall make their debts at the date of union less than $8,000,000 and $7,000,000 respectively, they shall be entitled to interest at 5 per cent. on the amount not so incurred, in like manner as is hereinafter provided for Newfoundland and Prince Edward Island; the foregoing resolution being in no respect intended to limit the powers given to the respective governments of those provinces by legislative authority, but only to limit the maximum amount of charge to be assumed by the general government: Provided always that the powers so conferred by the respective legislatures shall be exercised within five years from this date or the same shall then lapse.

    63. Newfoundland and Prince Edward Island, not having incurred debts equal to those of the other provinces, shall be entitled to receive by half-yearly payments in advance from the general government the interest at 5 per cent. on the difference between the actual amount of their respective debts at the time of the union, and the average amount of indebtedness per head of the population of Canada, Nova Scotia, and New Brunswick.

64. In consideration of the transfer to the general parliament of the powers of taxation, an annual grant in aid of each province shall be made, equal to 80 cents per head of the population, as established by the census of 1861, the population of Newfoundland being estimated at 130,000. Such aid shall be in full settlement of all future demands upon the general government for local purposes, and shall be paid half-yearly in advance to each province.

65. The position of New Brunswick being such as to entail large immediate charges upon her local revenues, it is agreed that for the period of ten years from the time when the union takes effect, an additional allowance of $63,000 per annum shall be made to that province; but that so long as the liability of that province remains under $7,000,000, a deduction equal to the interest on such deficiency shall be made from the $63,000.

66. In consideration of the surrender to the general government by Newfoundland of all its rights in mines and minerals, and of all the ungranted and unoccupied lands of the Crown, it is agreed that the sum of $150,000 shall each year be paid to that province, by semi-annual payments: Provided that that colony shall retain the right of opening, constructing, and controlling roads and bridges through any of the said lands, subject to any laws which the general parliament may pass in respect of the same.

67. All engagements that may, before the union, be entered into with the Imperial government for the defence of the country shall be assumed by the general government.

68. The general government shall secure, without delay, the completion of the intercolonial railway from Rivière-du-Loup through New Brunswick to Truro in Nova Scotia.

69. The communications with the North-Western territory, and the improvements required for the development of the trade of the Great West with the seaboard, are regarded by this Conference as subjects of the highest importance to the federated provinces, and shall be prosecuted at the earliest possible period that the state of the finances will permit.

70. The sanction of the Imperial and local parliaments shall be sought for the union of the provinces, on the principles adopted by the Conference.

71. That Her Majesty the Queen be solicited to determine the rank and name of the federated provinces.

72. The proceedings of the Conference shall be authenticated by the signatures of the delegates, and submitted by each delegation to its own government; and the Chairman is authorised to submit a copy to the Governor General for transmission to the Secretary of State for the Colonies.

COPIES OF OFFICIAL CORRESPONDENCE ON THE CONFEDERATION OF THE BRITISH NORTH AMERICAN PROVINCES, CANADIAN DEFENCES, HUDSON BAY TERRITORY, &c.

(No. 83.)—*Copy of a Despatch from Governor-General* VISCOUNT MONCK *to the Right Hon.* EDWARD CARDWELL, M.P.

QUEBEC: *March* 24, 1865.

Sir,—I have the honour to transmit for your information a copy of an approved minute of the Executive Council of Canada appointing a deputation from their body, who are to proceed to England to confer with Her

Majesty's Government on subjects of importance to the province.

The gentlemen named on the deputation propose leaving by the steamer which sails on the 5th of April.

I have, &c.
MONCK.

The Right Hon. EDWARD CARDWELL, M.P. &c.

(Enclosures in No. 1.)

(No. 95.)—*Copy of a Report of a* COMMITTEE OF THE HON. EXECUTIVE COUNCIL, *approved by His Excellency the Governor General on the 24th of March,* 1865.

The Committee respectfully recommend that four members of your Excellency's Council do proceed to England to confer with Her Majesty's Government—

1. Upon the proposed confederation of the British North American Provinces and the means whereby it can be most speedily effected.

2. Upon the arrangements necessary for the defence of Canada in the event of war arising with the United States, and the extent to which the same should be shared between Great Britain and Canada.

3. Upon the steps to be taken with reference to the Reciprocity Treaty and the rights conferred by it upon the United States.

4. Upon the arrangements necessary for the settlement of the North-West territory and Hudson's Bay Company's claims.

5. And generally upon the existing critical state of affairs, by which Canada is most seriously affected.

The Committee further recommend that the following members of Council be named to form a delegation, viz.: Messrs. Macdonald, Cartier, Brown, and Galt.

 Certified.   W. H. LEE, C.E.C.

(No. 2.)

(95.)—*Copy of a Despatch from the Right Hon.* EDWARD CARDWELL, *M.P., to Governor-General* VISCOUNT MONCK.

       DOWNING STREET: *June* 17, 1865.

My Lord,—I have the honour to inform your Lordship that several conferences have been held between the four Canadian Ministers who were deputed, under the minute of your Executive Council of March 24, to proceed to England to confer with Her Majesty's Government on the part of Canada, and the Duke of Somerset, the Earl de Grey, Mr. Gladstone, and myself on the part of Her Majesty's Government.

On the first subject referred to in the minute, that of the confederation of the British North American Provinces, we repeated on the part of the Cabinet the assurances which had already been given of the determination of Her Majesty's Government to use every proper means of influence to carry into effect without delay the proposed confederation.

On the second point we entered into a full consideration of the important subject of the defence of Canada, not with any apprehension on either side that the friendly relations now happily subsisting between this country and the United States are likely to be disturbed, but impressed with the conviction that the safety of the empire from possible attack ought to depend upon its own strength and the due application of its own resources. We reminded the Canadian Ministers that, on the part of the Imperial Government, we had obtained a vote of money for improving the fortifications of Quebec. We assured them that so soon as that vote had been obtained the necessary instructions had been sent out for the immediate execution of the works, which would be prosecuted with despatch; and we reminded them of the suggestion Her Majesty's Government had made to them to proceed with the fortifications of Montreal.

The Canadian Ministers, in reply, expressed unreservedly the desire of Canada to devote her whole resources, both in men and money, for the maintenance of her connection with the mother-country, and their full belief in the readiness of the Canadian Parliament to make known that determination in the most authentic manner. They said they had increased the expenditure for their militia from $300,000 to $1,000,000, and would agree to train that force to the satisfaction of the Secretary of State for War, provided the cost did not exceed the last-mentioned sum annually while the question of confederation is pending. They said they were unwilling to separate the question of the works of Montreal from the question of the works west of that place, and from the question of a naval armament in Lake Ontario. That the execution of the whole of these works would render it necessary for them to have recourse to a loan, which could only be raised with the guarantee of the Imperial Parliament. They were ready to propose to their Legislature on their return a measure for this purpose, provided that the guarantee of the Imperial Parliament were given now, and that they were authorised to communicate to the Parliament of Canada the assurance that, the occasion arising, England will have prepared an adequate naval force for Lake Ontario. They thought that if the guarantee were not obtained now, it was probable that the Canadian Government and Parliament would think it desirable that the question of defensive works should await the decision of the Government and Legislature of the United Provinces.

On the part of Her Majesty's Government we assented to the reasonableness of the proposal that if the province undertook the primary liability for the works of defence mentioned in the letter of Lieutenant-Colonel Jervois, and showed a sufficient security, Her Majesty's Government should apply to Parliament for a guarantee for the amount required; and we said that Her Majesty's Government would furnish the armaments for the works; but we said that the desire and decision of the Provincial Legislature ought to be pronounced before any application was made to the Imperial Parliament. On the subject of a naval force for Lake Ontario, we said that, apart from any question of expediency, the convention subsisting between this country and the United States rendered it impossible for either nation to place more than the specified number of armed vessels on the lakes in times of peace. In case of war it would, as a matter of course, be the duty of any government in this country to apply its means of naval defence according to the judgment it might form upon the exigencies of each particular time, and the Canadian Ministers might be assured that Her Majesty's Government would not permit itself to be found in such a position as to be unable to discharge its duty in this respect.

This was the only assurance the Canadian Ministers could expect or we could give.

Upon a review of the whole matter, the Canadian Ministers reverted to the proposal which has been mentioned above, that priority in point of time should be given to the confederation of the provinces. To this we, on the part of Her Majesty's Government, assented. In conformity, however, with a wish strongly expressed by the Canadian Ministers, we further said that if, upon future consideration, the Canadian Government should desire to anticipate the confederation, and to propose that Canada should execute the works, they would doubtless communicate to Her Majesty's Government that decision; and we trusted that after what had passed in these conferences they would feel assured that any such communication would be received by us in the most friendly spirit.

On the third point, the Reciprocity Treaty, the Canadian Ministers represented the great importance to Canada of the renewal of that treaty, and requested that Sir F. Bruce might be put in communication with the Government of Lord Monck upon the subject. We replied that Sir F. Bruce had already received instructions to negotiate for a renewal of the treaty and to act in concert with the Government of Canada.

On the fourth point, the subject of the North-Western territory, the Canadian Ministers desired that that territory should be made over to Canada, and undertook to negotiate with the Hudson's Bay Company for the termination of their rights, on condition that the indemnity, if any, should be paid by a loan to be raised by Canada under the Imperial guarantee. With the sanction of the Cabinet we assented to this proposal, undertaking that if the negotiation should be successful, we, on the part of the Crown, being satisfied that the amount of the indemnity was reasonable and the security sufficient, would apply to the Imperial Parliament to sanction the arrangement and to guarantee the amount.

On the last point, it seemed sufficient that Her Majesty's Government should accept the assurances given by the Canadian Ministers on the part of Canada, that that province is ready to devote all her resources, both in men and money, to the maintenance of her connection with the mother-country, and should assure them in return that the Imperial Government fully acknowledged the reciprocal obligation of defending every portion of the empire with all the resources at its command.

The Canadian Ministers, in conclusion, said that they hoped it would be understood that the present communications did not in any way affect or alter the correspondence which had already passed between the Imperial Government and the Governments of the British North American provinces on the subject of the Intercolonial Railway. To this we entirely agreed.

I have, &c.
EDWARD CARDWELL.

APPENDIX B.

Summary of the Constitution of the United States referred to, p. 48.

Article I.

SECTION

1. All legislative power is vested in a Congress, consisting of a Senate and House of Representatives.
2. Composition of House of Representatives—chosen every second year.
3. Senate composed of two senators from each State, chosen by the legislatures thereof for six years; age 30 years.
4. Manner of elections for senators—Congress to assemble once every year.
5. Privileges of each house.
6. Compensation to senators and representatives; their privileges.
7. Bills for raising revenue originate in House of Representatives—veto of President.
8. Power of Congress.—1. To levy taxes; 2. Borrow money; 3. Regulate commerce; 4. Naturalization and National Bank; 5. Coin money; 7. Post-office; 11. Declare war; 12. Raise and support armies; 13. A navy; 15. Militia.
10. What each State cannot do: not enter into any treaty—coin money—or levy impost or duty on imports.

Article II.

SECTION

1.—1. Executive power in President—holds office for four years; 2. Manner of electing President and Vice-President—each State to choose electors equal to its whole number of senators and representatives in Congress; 3. Manner of voting by elections—President to have the majority of electors; 4. Natural born citizens alone can be President.

2.—1. President Commander-in-Chief of the army and navy; 2. Can make treaties by and with the consent of the Senate.

Article III.

1. Judicial power vested in a supreme court, and in such inferior courts as Congress may establish—judges hold office during good behaviour.
2. To what cases judicial power to extend.

Article IV.

1. Full faith and credit shall be given in each State to the public Acts, &c. of other States.
2. Citizens of each State entitled to privileges, &c. in other States—(relation of States to each other).
3. New States admitted.

Article V.

Congress by 2-3rds vote may amend constitution.

Article VI.

1. Debts before constitution adopted—to be valid against United States.
2. Constitution, supreme law of land.

Article VII.

Ratification of constitution by nine States sufficient.

AMENDMENTS TO THE CONSTITUTION.

Article X.

Powers not delegated to the United States by the constitution, nor prohibited by it to the States, are reserved to the States respectively, or to the people.

APPENDIX C.

Expenditure, including cost of barracks, fortifications, and transportations incurred in defence of dependencies, also number and distribution of troops (Select Com. 1861).

Colonies Proper	Infantry of the Line	Colonial Infantry	Artillery	Engineers	Totals	Imperial Military Expenditure	
Canada	1,039	1,137	248	8	2,432	£206,264	
Nova Scotia and New Brunswick	1,612	...	177	92	1,881*	149,495	
Newfoundland	...	237	1	1	239	20,807	
British Columbia	...	...	...	138	138	37,000	
							£413,566
New South Wales	507	...	106	32	645	43,039	
Victoria	618	...	...	6	624	36,557	
South Australia	93	...	...	7	100	6,836	
Tasmania	324	...	...	2	326	35,113	
New Zealand	1,166	...	45	41	1,252	104,852	
							226,347
Cape of Good Hope, Natal, & Kaffraria	3,409	1,042	176	239	4,866	456,658	
Ceylon	846	1,356	135	7	2,344	110,268	
Mauritius	1,449	...	133	48	1,630	145,658	
West Indies.							
Jamaica	534	802	94	3	1,433	118,285	
Honduras	...	329	24	2	355	30,621	
Windward and Leeward Islands	1,145	1,104	136	7	2,399	213,793	
							1,075,273
Totals	12,741	6,007	1,275	633	20,657	£1,715,246	
Imperial Garrisons.							
Malta	5,008	637	779	306	6,728	483,173	
Gibraltar	4,537	...	1,079	309	5,925	420,695	
Ionian Islands	3,601	...	487	206	4,294	280,061	
Hong Kong	...	...	...	...	733	57,300	
St. Helena	...	418	77	2	497	38,354	
Bermuda	878	...	159	91	1,128	87,587	
Bahamas	...	388	11	1	398	32,280	
Falkland	...	37	...	...	37	2,117	
West Australia	88	...	...	56	174	25,946	
Labuan	...	...	...	...	...	7,329	
West Africa	...	356	...	...	356	27,302	
Sierra Leone	...	334	...	...	334	27,990	
Gambia, Gold Coast	...	306	...	...	306	19,781	
Totals	14,112	2,474	2,592	999	20,910	£1,509,835	
							£3,225,081

* 1,300 of these were in the Imperial garrison of Halifax.

APPENDIX D.

STATISTICS OF AUSTRALIAN COLONIES.

The last Census was taken in 1861, with a view of according with the Census time of the United Kingdom. The following are the chief features of that year:—

Subject	Queensland	New South Wales	Victoria	South Australia	West Australia	Tasmania	New Zealand
Population	34,367	358,278	540,322	130,627	15,691	90,211	106,315
Imports	£967,951	£6,391,551	£13,532,452	£1,976,018	£147,913	£1,054,517	£2,493,811
Exports	709,599	5,594,839	13,828,606	2,032,311	95,789	905,463	1,370,247
Ordinary Revenue	238,239	1,421,831	3,055,522	575,576	67,261	316,733	691,464
Public Debt	...	4,017,630	6,285,060	850,500	...	450,000	500,000
1863							
Population	61,640	378,939	574,331	140,416	18,700	91,519	
Imports	£1,713,263	£8,319,576	...	£2,028,279	£140,003	£902,940	
Exports	888,381	6,936,839	£2,722,299	2,358,817	111,754	999,511	
Revenue	404,720	...	9,000,000	639,700	54,480	252,489	
Debt	123,700	...		...	...	497,738	
1864							
Population	...	...	604,858	...	...	...	
Imports	...	...	£14,409,028	...	...	...	£707,974
Exports	...	...	13,850,898	...	...	...	1,650,000
Revenue	£524,199	...	2,851,712	...	...	...	
Debt	698,000	...	9,000,000	...	...	...	

NORTH AMERICAN COLONIES.

	Upper Canada	Lower Canada	Nova Scotia	New Brunswick	Newfoundland	Prince Edward's	Totals
1864							
Population	1,650,000	1,225,800	349,300	272,780	137,800	85,992	3,644,672
Population	2,876,800						
Revenue, 1863	*$9,760,316		$1,185,629	$899,991	$480,000	$197,384	$12,523,320
Expenditure	10,742,807		1,072,274	884,613	479,420	171,718	13,350,832
Debt, loss, Sinking Fund	60,365,472		4,858,547	5,702,991	946,000	240,573	72,103,583
1864			1863	1863	1863	1863	
Imports	$52,498,066		$10,201,391	$7,764,824	$5,242,724	$1,428,028	$70,601,460
Duty	6,637,503						
Per-centage on imports	12¾ per cent.						
1863							
Exports	$41,831,632		$8,420,968	$8,964,784	$6,002,212	$1,627,540	$66,847,036
Duties	Canada		861,988	767,354†	483,460	145,302	7,427,528
Population per square mile	5,169,173		18·12	10·06	3·41	40·95	Average, 8·32
Revenue, per head	8·40		$3·39	$3·29	$3·50	$2·29	„ $3·45
Debt, per head	$3·51		13·91	20·91	6·90	2·79	„ 19·83
	21·09						

* Increase in 1864, $1,500,000, leaving a surplus in Canada ; and in all the provinces of $872,000.
† Also export duty on timber, $68,631.

APPENDIX E.

BRITISH COLONIES.

Names	Mode of Acquisition	Date	Population	Date of Return	
Anguilla	Settlement	1650	4,000	1860	
Antigua	,,	1632 }	36,593	1861	
Barbuda	,,	1628 }			
Ascension	,,	1827			
Bahamas	,,	1629	35,287	1861	
Barbadoes	,,	1625	152,262	1861	
Berbece	Capture	1803	27,003	1851	
Bermuda	Settlement	1609	11,092	1851	
Columbia, British	,,	1858	10,000	1862	
Kaffraria	Separated from Cape of Good Hope	1860			
Canada, East } Canada, West }	Cession	1763	3,000,000 (nearly)	1864	Quebec captured 1759, cession 1763, settlement of Canada West 1783.
Cape Breton	Capture and cession	1713	63,000	1861	
Cape of Good Hope	Capture	1806	300,000	1860	
Ceylon	,,	1795	1,876,467	1860	
Demerara and Essequibo	,,	1803	100,000	1851	
Dominica	Cession	1763	25,200	1861	
Falkland Islands	Settlement	1842	500	1855	
Gambia	,,	1631	6,693	1861	
Gibraltar	Capture	1704	17,642	1860	
Gold Coast	Settlement	1661	400,000	1851	
Gold Coast (late Danish)	Cession	1850			
Grenada	,,	1763	31,900	1861	
Guiana	Capitulation	1803	148,026	1861	
Heligoland	Cession	1814	2,000	1861	
Honduras	,, Settlement	1670 } 1742 }	25,631	1861	
Hong Kong	Cession	1842	94,917	1860	
Jamaica	Capture	1655	441,253	1861	
Labuan	Cession	1846	2,373	1861	

APPENDIX.

BRITISH COLONIES—*continued.*

Names	Mode of Acquisition	Date	Population	Date of Return	
Lagos	Constituted a colony	1862			
Malta, Gozo, and Comino	Capture	1800	136,496	1861	
Mauritius	,,	1810	307,212	1861	
Montserrat	Settlement	1632	7,654	1861	
Natal	,,	1824	157,583	,,	
Nevis	,,	1628	10,200	1861	
New Brunswick	,, Separated from Nova Scotia	1783 1784	252,047	1861	
Newfoundland	Settlement	1608	122,638	1861	
New South Wales	,,	1788	378,934	1863	
New Zealand	,,	1839	106,204	1861	
Norfolk Island	,, Resettlement Transferred to Pitcairn Islanders	1788 1825 1856	185	1856	
Nova Scotia	Capture and cession	1713	330,857	1861	
Prince Edward's Island	,, ,,	1713	80,757	,,	
Queensland	Separated from New South Wales	1859	61,640	1863	
St. Christopher	Settlement	1623	24,742	1861	
St. Helena	Cession Transferred to Government	1673 1836	6,860	1861	
St. Lucia	Capture	1803	26,713	1861	
St. Vincent	Cession	1763	30,128	1861	
Sierra Leone	Settlement Transferred to Government	1789 1807	44,801	1851	
South Australia	Settlement	1836	130,000	1861	
Tasmania	,,	1804	89,977	1861	
Tobago	Cession	1763	15,410	1861	
Trinidad	Capture	1797	84,432	1861	
Tristan D'Acunha	Settlement	1818	90	1845	
Turks and Caicos	,,	...	4,372	1861	
Vancouver's Island	,,	1781	23,000	1862	Sta. ab. 1863.
Victoria	Settlement Separated from New South Wales	1836 1850	604,000	1864	
Virgin Islands	Settlement	1666	6,053	1859	
West Australia	,,	1829	15,593	1861	

APPENDIX F.

IMPORTS AND EXPORTS PER HEAD OF POPULATION.

Name of Colony	Population, 1861	Exports, 1861	Imports, 1861	Amount of Imports per head of Population			Imports, 1864
		£	£	£	s.	d.	£
Canada	2,500,000	7,523,465	8,846,884	3	10	9	9,986,431
New Brunswick	252,047	947,091	1,238,133	4	18	0	1,291,604
Nova Scotia	330,857	1,154,867	1,525,645	4	12	0	1,689,008
Newfoundland	122,638	1,092,555	1,152,857	9	10	0	1,007,082
New South Wales	350,860	5,594,839	6,391,555	18	0	0	9,334,645
South Australia	126,830	2,032,311	1,976,018	15	10	0	1,820,656
Victoria	540,671	13,828,606	13,532,452	25	10	0	13,487,787
West Australia	15,593	95,789	147,913	9	0	0	172,991
Queensland	34,367	709,599	967,951	28	0	0	1,323,509
Tasmania	89,977	905,463	954,517	10	14	0	857,423
New Zealand	135,000	1,370,247	2,493,811	18	9	0	4,624,082

United States, 30,000,000, imported in 1859 from Great Britain, 17s. only per head of population . . . 0 17 0
The British Colonies, in 1861, imported from Great Britain . . . . . per head 5 5 0

APPENDIX G.

Emigration from the United Kingdom to the United States and British Colonies from the year 1815 to 1864.

Years	United States	North American Colonies	Australia and New Zealand Colonies	All other places	Totals
1815 to 1846	780,048	746,163	124,342	21,603	1,672,156
1847*	142,154	109,680	4,949	1,487	258,270
1848	188,233	31,065	23,904	4,887	248,089
1849	219,450	41,367	32,191	6,490	299,498
1850	223,078	32,961	16,037	8,773	280,849
1851	267,357	42,605	21,532	4,472	335,966
1852	244,261	32,873	†87,881	3,749	368,764
1853	230,885	34,522	61,401	3,129	329,937
1854	193,065	43,761	83,237	3,366	323,429
1855	103,414	17,966	52,309	3,118	176,807
1856	111,837	16,378	44,584	3,755	176,554
1857	126,905	21,001	61,248	3,721	212,875
1858	59,716	9,704	39,295	5,257	113,972
1859	70,303	6,689	31,013	12,427	120,432
1860	87,500	9,786	24,302	6,881	128,469
1861	49,764	12,707	23,738	5,561	91,770
1862	58,706	15,522	41,843	5,143	121,214
1863	146,813	18,083	53,054	5,808	223,758
1864	147,042	12,721	40,942	8,195	208,900
Total	3,450,531	1,255,554	867,802	117,822	5,691,709

Total Emigration from Great Britain from 1815 to 1864 . 5,691,709
" " to British Colonies 2,123,356
" " United States 3,450,530

* Irish famine, £10,000,000 granted.
† Australian gold discoveries.

APPENDIX H.

COLONIAL OFFICE.

In the reign of George III. 1768, a Secretary of State for the American, or Colonial Department, was appointed, in addition to the two principal Secretaries of State then existing. In 1782 the duties of the two principal Secretaries of State were divided into 'Home' and 'Foreign,' the affairs of Ireland and the Colonies devolving on the Home Department. In 1794 a principal Secretary for War was appointed, and the affairs of the Colonies were transferred to the War Department in 1801. In 1854 a fourth principal Secretary of State was added, the affairs of the Colonies alone being placed under one Secretary.

Officers of State who have been Secretaries for the Colonies from 1768 to 1865, with the dates of their Appointments.

SECRETARIES FOR THE AMERICAN OR COLONIAL DEPARTMENT.

1768. Feb. 27th	. .	Earl of Hillsborough.
1772. Aug. 27th	. .	William, Earl of Dartmouth.
1776. Jan. 25th	. .	Lord George Sackville Germaine.

SECRETARIES FOR HOME (FORMERLY AMERICAN OR COLONIAL) DEPARTMENT.

1782. March 27th	.	William, Earl Shelbourne.
1782. July 17th	. .	Thomas, Lord Grantham.
1783. April 2nd	. .	Frederick, Lord North.

APPENDIX.

1783. Dec. 23rd . . Francis, Marquis of Carmarthen.
1789. Jan. 5th . . . Right Hon. W. Windham Grenville.
1794. July 11th . . Right Hon. Henry Dundas (Lord Melville).

SECRETARIES FOR WAR AND COLONIES.

1801. March 17th . Robert, Lord Hobart.
1804. May 12th . . John, Earl Camden.
1805. July 10th . . Robert, Viscount Castlereagh.
1806. Feb. 14th . . Right Hon. William Windham.
1807. March 15th . Robert, Viscount Castlereagh.
1809. Oct. 11th . . Robert Banks, Earl of Liverpool.
1812. Jan. 11th . . Henry, Earl of Bathurst.
1827. April 30th . . Right Hon. William Robinson.
1827. Aug. 17th . . Right Hon. William Huskisson.
1828. May 20th . . Right Hon. Sir George Murray.
1830. Nov. 20th . . Viscount Goderich.
1833. April . . . . Right Hon. E. G. S. Stanley (Earl Derby).
1834. June 5th . . Right Hon. Thomas Spring Rice (Lord Monteagle).
1834. Dec. 20th . . George, Earl of Aberdeen.
1835. April 18th . . Right Hon. Charles Grant (Lord Glenelg).
1839. Feb. 20th . . Constantine Henry, Marquis of Normandy.
1839. Aug. 31st . . Lord John Russell (Earl Russell).
1841. Sept. 3rd . . Lord Stanley (Earl Derby).
1845. Dec. 23rd . . Right Hon. W. E. Gladstone.
1846. July 6th . . . Henry, Earl Grey.
1852. Feb. 27th . . Right Hon. Sir Joseph Pakington, Bart.
1852. Dec. 28th . . Henry Pelham, Duke of Newcastle.

SECRETARIES FOR THE COLONIES.

1854. June 12th . . Right Hon. Sir George Grey, Bart.
1855. Feb. 8th . . . Right Hon. Sidney Herbert (Lord Herbert of Lea).
1855. May 15th . . Lord John Russell (Earl Russell).
1855. July 21st . . Right Hon. Sir W. Molesworth, Bart.
1855. Nov. 17th . . Right Hon. Henry Labouchere (Lord Taunton).
1858. Feb. 26th . . Lord Stanley.
1858. May 31st . . Right Hon. Sir E. Bulwer Lytton, Bart.
1859. June 18th . . Duke of Newcastle.
1864. April 4th . . Right Hon. Edward Cardwell.

INDEX.

ADDERLEY on Canada, 142. Object of his pamphlet, 147. Review of pamphlet, 150. On policy of old and new colonies, 160

Advantages of colonies, 114. Trade with, 118

American Colonization, two centres of, Virginia and New England, 2

American Republic, errors of, 48–52. As an aggressive power, 108. Balance of power on American continent, 110

Aristocracies in Europe, 140

Australia, responsible government conceded, 44. Free-trade and protection, 68–9. Trade of, 93–4, 118, 122. Threatened, 130. Trade of, and its protection, 175. Defence of, 182–3. Volunteers in, 192. People of, 193. Convict question, 207. Marvellous development of, 215. Compared with United States, 217

BALANCE of power in America and Europe, 110

Blackstone's division of colonies, 9–11

British America, 36. Loyalty of, 36. Confederation of, 47–56. Meeting at Charlottetown, 47. At Quebec, 48 (Appendix A). Articles of Confederation, 48–55. Compared with constitution of United States, 48, 52. Evidences of compromises, 50. Central and local governments, 51, 53. Triple governments, local, federal, and Imperial, 52. Legislative Council or nominated Chamber, little influence of, 53–4. Power of the Crown to disallow, 54–5. Composition of the two Houses, 55. Lower Canada, the pivot, 55. Trade of, 93–4. Vast results, 94

British North America, volunteers in, 192. Marine of, 200. Population, trade, revenue, debt, 215, 257. Immigration to, 261

Brodie, W., on the claims New Zealand has on England in native wars, 137. Colonial militia better than English troops, 190. English Government manages native affairs, 190

Burgoyne, General Sir John. Basis of England's calculations, 177. Troops in Kingston, Quebec, and Halifax, 178. Vote for a citadel at Halifax, 178. Opinions on Mr. Godley's views, 178. Enemies opposed to old colonies, few, 178. Trifling expenses for Kingston and Quebec, 178

Burke, Edmund, 39

CANADA.—Capture of Quebec, 37. Responsible government, 37–46. Resolutions of 1841, 37.

CAN

Conceded, 44. Effect of, 44–6. The vacillating commercial policy of England, 66. Revenue laws of Canada, 68–75. Proportion of customs in Canada and England, 73. Customs in England and Canada, 75, 80. Could not adopt free-trade, 82. Call for protection, 86. Its effect in peace and in war, 87. Trade of, 93, 118, 122. A source of weakness or strength to England, 95. Character of population, 96. Proofs of loyalty, 97. Defence of Canada is defence of Br. America, 110, 123. Colonel Jervois' Report, 123. Debate on, in the House of Commons, 123. *Casus Belli*, come from the sea, and not from colonies, 127. Position of contrasted with England, 130. Why sending troops to, 134, 152, 173. Paying troops in, 137. During the American war, 141. Trent affair, 142, 201. Abolition of slavery in the States, what influence on Canada, 145. Military spirit of, 148. Gladstone on, 149. Clergy, how paid, 154. Lord Herbert on military force in, 176. Position of, in war of 1812, 185. Earl Derby on, 201. Growth of, in comparison with United States, 217. Settlement, 37, 258. Defence, 255. Population, trade, revenue, debt, &c., 257

Canadian ministers, delegation to the Home Government, 247.

Cape Colony, wars of, 136, 138. Government responsible, 183.

Capital and labour in colonies, 115

Cardwell, Right Hon. Edward, Colonial Secretary, despatch of, on confederation and defence of British North America, 125, 247

Carthage, its colonies, 26. Commercial policy and government, 26

COL

Casus Belli, whence they arise, 127

Charter governments, 10. Nature of first, 18, 33. Last of, 33

Chatham, Lord, on the right of Parliament to tax colonies, 63–4–5. Profits to Britain from trade of colonies, 114

Church, first in New England, 6. Oath of supremacy in, attempts to establish church, 21

Colonial governments, ancient and modern, 18–35. Greek, 25. Tyrian, 25. Carthagenian, 26. Roman, 27. Around shores of Mediterranean, in Europe, in America, 22–35. Contrast between ancient and modern, 28–9. Portugal, 27. Spain, 30. Holland, 30. France, 31. The earth divided between Portugal and Spain, 29–30. Disputes with the Crown and Parliament, 33–35. Parliamentary governments in colonies, 36–46. Interference with by Russell's ministry, 43. 'Times' on direct and indirect taxation, 83. On political and moral effects of income-tax, 84

Colonies, so numerous and varied that no rigid rule can be laid down for all, 56–7. Duty of, in defence, volunteers, 58. No British colonies conquered, none involved England in war, 58–9. Will England go to war on colonial questions? 58–9. Character of colonial population, 59. Volunteer system, 59–60. Classification of, 89. Source of weakness or strength, 95. Expenditure on colonial account, 98. For what purposes, 99. What advantages to colonies to remain part of the empire, 111. What to mother country, 113. Field for emigration, 115, 121. Colonies England's best customers, 118, 120. Trade with, 120, 122. What binds them to England?—

COL

is it interest, 129. Sons of enter army and navy, 131. Teachers of constitutional government, 132. Do they draw England into war, 133. Why Democratic, 140. Modern colonies differ from the old in their policy, 147. Imperial policy and colonial opinions, 155. Imperial interests, how represented in colonies and colonial in England, 156. Policy of old and new, 160. Why old colonies refused English troops, 160. Demanded troops to be placed under their own control, any why, 163. Feared Parliament, and never submitted to it, 164. Troops in, 99, 173, 176. Colonies often denuded of troops, 177. Moral and social tie with, the valuable one, 180. Obligation to defend, 186. Barracks in, 182. Position of old different from the new, 183. Never attacked by great armies of civilized Powers, 184. French troops in Canada, few, 184. England's foreign policy and defence of colonies, 193. Effect of sending soldiers to, 193. Future of, 195-222. As allies, 196. As maritime States, 200. Loyalty of old colonies, 203-7. British America and Australia, 207. Basis of union with England, 208. Trade of, 215. Independence of, 216. Growth of, 217. As fields for surplus population of England, 214. Relation of old colonies to England suggests basis of union, 221. Influence of commerce in home and foreign policy, 222. To England would belong chief advantage of such union, 222. Immigration, 261

Commerce, influence in the policy of the nation, 222

Commercial policy, Carthage, 26 Commercial monopoly of Portugal, 29. Of Holland, 31, 61.

DEM

Of England, 34. Navigation Acts of 1651 and 1703, 62-65. Effect of, 65. Modifications of, 66. Free-trade in England, 67, 72, 75. Earl Grey on free-trade in colonies, 70. Instructions to Governor of New Brunswick, 71. England and Canada, 75. England raises two-thirds of revenue by indirect taxation, and not one-sixth by direct, 76. Foreign produce pays £24,000,000 at British ports before admitted to British markets, 76. Gladstone on free-trade and revenue, 77-9. New countries without manufactures, in war, 87. Protection and free-trade in Australia, 68-9. In Canada, 86

Commonwealth of England founded the restrictive commercial policy, 62

Confederation of British America; its population, area, resources, 212-15. Trade of, 215

Confederation of old colonies, from 1643—1790, 12-18. Objects and nature of, 12. Assumed the functions of an independent government, 13. General Congress in 1765, 13. Continental Congress, 14. Second Congress from all the States, 15. Articles of, ratified, 16. Defects, 16, 17. New constitution of United States, 17 (Appendix B). Confederation of British America, 47-56

Cost of colonies, 89-128. Report of Committee of House of Commons, 89. For navy, 94. 'Times' on, 150. Cost of defence, how to be borne, 157. Mr. Merivale on, 158. Duke of Newcastle on, 159. Earl Grey, 159.

DECLARATION of rights, 13, 14, 15

Democracy in the first colonies, 4, 7, 8, 22

Derby, Earl, on attitude of Canada, when British flag was insulted, 201

Disraeli on the defence of Canada, 126

Dufferin, Lord, on the loyalty of Canada, 202

ELLIOT, F., importance of Halifax, garrisoned for Imperial purposes, 191

England, colonial policy of, 56–61, Responsible for foreign relations, 57–8. Fears cost, and commerce, 59. England, agricultural and manufacturing, 87. Which has the chief influence in causing war, England or her colonies, 133. English and French policy, as a peace policy, 135. Has tried to establish her institutions, civil and ecclesiastical, in colonies, 139. Relations to slave-holding States, 146. England and France, 149. Colonial policy, 151. The power of England and her colonies united, 198. If not united, whose fault; 200. Basis of union, 208, 221. Position of old colonies, 221

Erskine, Rear-Admiral, evidence of, on maintaining garrisons, 192

FRANCE, colonies of, 31. Policy of, in Europe and America, 134. As a peace policy, 135. Navy of, 199

Franchise, extension of in England, and its effects upon her colonial policy, 211. The class that would dictate policy of the empire, 211. In England and the colonies, how it differs, 200. Seventy per cent. of population in colonies owners of the land they vote on, 209. In England the reverse, 209–10. Demand in colonies to raise the qualification, 211. In England to lower it, 210. Complaints as to the class that dictate the policy of the empire, 211

Franklin, Dr., 16. In House of Commons, 34, 63

Free-trade in England, 67. (See Commercial Policy.) In the abstract, 76, 81. Gladstone on, 77–9. A policy and not a truth, 84–5

GARRISONS, 90. Defence of, 182. Halifax same as Malta and Gibraltar, 182, 191. Cost of troops in, 185. Effect on colonies, 185. Admiral Erskine's evidence on, 192

Gladstone, Hon. W. E., obligation of mother country, 178. What system best, 179. Old colonies and Canada, 179. Military spirit in Canada, 179. In old colonies, 180. Ignorance of colonial affairs, 180. Moral and social tie the valuable one, 180. Colonies safe while England is supreme at sea, 181. Old colonies and new, 181

Gladstone on free-trade and revenue, 77–9. Who pays malt-tax and customs, 79. False position, 81

Glenelg's, Lord, despatch to Sir Francis Head, on rights of local governments, 1839, 43, 72

Governments, 4, 5, 9, 10. Representative, 2, 3. Provincial, proprietary, and charter, 9–11. Colonial governments, municipal only, 10–11. Difference in Massachusetts, Connecticut, and Rhode Island, 12. First general, in colonies, origin of, 14, 15. First American, independent of Parliament, 18. Relation to the Crown, 18. Repealed common and statute law, 19, 20. Repudiated Acts of Parliament, 20. Disputed authority of King's Commissioners, 20. Represen-

tative, 22–28. Self-government in Europe, 25. Colonial governments, nature of, 25–35. Responsible government conceded, 44. Effects of, 44–6. United States and British America, 48–52. Republics of America, 49. Blunders in government of old colonies, 56. No one rigid rule applicable to all, 56–7
Godley, J. R., evidence of, on duties of Imperial and colonial Governments, 187–8. Recommends Sir W. Denison's plan and Earl Grey's policy, 187, 189
Grenville, Lord, 64
Greek colonies, 25
Grey, Earl, on paying troops in Canada, 137. On wars at the Cape and in New Zealand, 138, 182. Obligation to defend colonies, 181. Grounds of such defence, 182. Barracks and garrisons in colonies, 182. Australian colonies, 182. Responsibility of England for wars at the Cape and New Zealand, 183. Old colonies, 831. Effect of withdrawing troops from New Zealand, 184. Old colonies never attacked by armies of civilized Powers, 184. Troops cost little more in colonies, 185, Canada in 1812, 185. In a war created by our colonial relations, 185. Profits of Dutch colonies, 186

HARTINGTON, Marquis of, on the defence of Canada, 123
Herbert, Lord, on keeping a military force in Canada, 176. Opposed to Mr. Lowe on keeping troops in colonies, 176. Troops in colonies in time of peace, 176. Colonies often denuded of troops, 177
Holland, profits from colonies, 186.

INDIA, protection in, 68

JERVOIS, Colonel, Report of, 123

LAING, Finance Minister of India, on direct and indirect taxation and free-trade, 73. Colonies our best customers, 118
Lowe, Right Hon. R., on keeping troops in New South Wales, 192–3. Colonies subject to England's foreign policy, 193. Australians as soldiers, 193. Effect of sending soldiers to colonies, 193

MANSFIELD, Lord, on right of franchise, 65
Maryland, first province of the empire, 32. Its acts not subject to veto by Crown, 32. Confers titles of honour, 32
Merivale, Herman (Under-Secretary for colonies for twelve years), on responsible government, 45. On effect of navigation laws, 65. Defence of commerce, 93. Colonial expenditure, 91, 98. On uniform rule as to defence of colonies, 172, 174. Different position of several colonies, 172–3. For what purposes troops are kept in colonies, 173. Case of Canada, 173. Confederation of North American provinces, 173. Occupation of Vancouver's an Imperial object, 174. An evil of administration, 174. No conclusion to be drawn from one colony as a guide to another, 175. Native affairs should be controlled by colony, 175. Trade of Australia and its protection, 175
Mills, Select Committee of 1861, 89
Monck, Viscount, Governor-General of British North America, despatch of, 245

NAVIGATION ACTS, 20. Of 1651 and 1763, 34

NEW

New Brunswick, 42. Differential duties and bounties, 42-3. Responsible government conceded, 44. Free-trade denied to, 68. Earl Grey on, 71. Assembly of, 72. Militia of, 185. Volunteers, 192. Settlement, 36, 259. Defence, 255. Population, trade, revenue, debt, &c., 257

New England, first settlers, 3. First government a pure Democracy, 4. Boundary, 5. Territory held of the Crown, 5. Government, nature of, and how elected, 5. Who were freemen, 6. Growth of the colony, 7. Contest with the Crown, 7. Loss of charter, 7. Without a charter from 1684-91, 8. Charter from William and Mary, 8

New South Wales, troops in, 192. Population, trade, revenue, debt, &c., 256. Settlement of, 215, 259. Cost of defence, 255

New Zealand, wars of, 136. Colonists' opinion on, 153. Warlike natives, 183. Effect of withdrawing troops, 184. Settlement, 259. Cost of defence, 255, Population, trade, revenue, debt, &c., 256

Newcastle, Duke of, on influence on Canada of the abolition of slavery in the States, 146, 170. On defence of colonies, 166. No rigid rule can be laid down, 167. Troops in Canada for convenience or for Imperial policy, 167. Halifax an Imperial port, 168. Superior to Bermuda, 168. Canada and Australia differently situated, 169. Confederation of the North American provinces, 169. Spirit of, 170. Canada not simply a cost to England, 171. Question of empire, 171

Newfoundland, volunteers in, 192. Settlement, 36, 259. Defence, 255. Population, trade, revenue, debt, &c., 257

RUS

Nova Scotia, conquest of, 105. Militia in, 155. Importance of Halifax, 191. Volunteers, 192. Settlement, 36, 259. Defence, 255. Population, trade, revenue, debt, &c., 257

PALMERSTON, Lord, on the defence of Canada, 125

Parliament, omnipotence of, 10, 11. Rights claimed, 33-35. Would not legislate, nor allow colonies to, 43. Tax colonies, 63.

Parliamentary government, see governments

Plymouth Colony, 4. Patent to, 4. New charter, 5. Incorporated with Massachusetts, 5

Population of colonies in America in 1660 and 1763, 13

Prince Edward's, first meeting on confederation of British America, 47. Settlement of, 259. Population, trade, &c., 257

Proprietary governments, 10

Provincial governments, 9, 10

QUEENSLAND, settlement, 259. Population, trade, revenue, debt, &c., 256. Cost of defence, 255

RELIGIOUS QUESTIONS, no reference to, in Massachusetts charters, 6.

Representative Government, first in America, 2, 3. Not provided for in first charter, 7, 8. One house, then two, 8, 18, 19, 22-28. In Europe, 25, 31, 35

Responsible government, see governments

Rhode Island and Connecticut, governments of, 21

Rome, how she enlarged her empire, 27. Military posts, 28

Russell, Earl, on responsible government, 40-1

S

SAN JUAN, 135
Settlements, first in America, 1. Growth of States, and their relation to England, 35
Ships, colonies, and commerce, express high interests of maritime States, 218
South Australia, settlement, 259. Population, trade, revenue, debt, &c., 256. Cost of defence, 255
Story, Judge, 20

T

TASMANIA, settlement, 259. Population, trade, revenue, debt, &c., 256. Defence, 255
Taxation of colonies, 34
'Times' on direct and indirect taxation, 83. On political and moral effects of income-tax, 84
Trade of colonies, 215
Trade with colonies and other countries, 118–19. Of Britain, in 1704, 122
Tyrian colonies, 25

U

UNITED STATES, growth of navy, 190. As colonies, as an independent State, 197

V

VANCOUVER'S, occupation of, an Imperial object, 174
Victoria, cost of defence, 255. Population, trade, revenue, debt, &c., 256
Virginia, settlement of, 1. First charters, 2. Written constitution, and nature of government, 3. The model of others, 3

W

WEST AUSTRALIA, settlement, 259. Defence, 255. Population, trade, revenue, debt, &c., 256

www.ingramcontent.com/pod-product-compliance
Lightning Source LLC
Chambersburg PA
CBHW032104230426
43672CB00009B/1640